A Student Guide to Writing an Undergraduate Psychology Honors Thesis

A Student Guide to Writing an Undergraduate Psychology Honors Thesis takes students through the entire process of creating a full-scale research project, from selecting a topic, to choosing an experimental or correlational design, to writing and presenting their paper.

The book offers valuable guidance on developing broader skills like communicating with your supervisor, time management, and critical writing skills. Chapters cover topics such as mentor selection, collecting journal articles, gathering and analyzing data, and writing a full APA or BPS experimental paper and will orientate and guide psychology students as they navigate the expected components of an honors thesis.

Designed for any student that is currently working on an independent research project, *A Student Guide to Writing an Undergraduate Psychology Honors Thesis* is the perfect companion for those working on their senior honors thesis in psychology.

Ross Seligman is currently an assistant adjunct professor at Pasadena City College. He has been teaching at various colleges for the past 30 years. His speciality is teaching Research Methods in Psychology and mentoring students on their independent research projects. During his academic career he has also been a tenured professor, worked as a department chair for eight years, and served as a dean for one year.

Lindsay Mitchell is currently a master's student attending Parker University. She is studying neuroscience and hopes to contribute to research in neural prosthesis and related topics. During her young adult life, Lindsay worked as a direct support professional for an individual with autism who inspired her future research interests. She aims to extend the use of neural prosthetics to similar individuals in the effort to enhance their day-to-day lives.

A Student Guide to Writing an Undergraduate Psychology Honors Thesis

Ross Seligman and Lindsay Mitchell

Routledge
Taylor & Francis Group

NEW YORK AND LONDON

First published 2023
by Routledge
605 Third Avenue, New York, NY 10158

and by Routledge
4 Park Square, Milton Park, Abingdon, Oxon, OX14 4RN

Routledge is an imprint of the Taylor & Francis Group, an informa business

© 2023 Ross Seligman and Lindsay Mitchell

Library of Congress Cataloging-in-Publication Data
A catalog record for this title has been requested

ISBN: 978-0-367-56809-2 (hbk)
ISBN: 978-0-367-56252-6 (pbk)
ISBN: 978-1-003-09940-6 (ebk)

DOI: 10.4324/9781003099406

Typeset in Bembo
by Apex CoVantage, LLC

Contents

Part I
Getting Started

1 Getting Started

Greetings! Your ambition has led you to pursue an undergraduate honors thesis in psychology. This puts you at the top of your game. The project that you will be completing in the next year will be a large project during which you will learn several new skills and be able to work alongside other talented researchers at your school. With that in mind, let's get started!

Introductions

I would like to start off with a couple of introductions. My name is Ross Seligman and I have been teaching psychology at various colleges for the past 30 years. I specialize in teaching research methods and mentoring students as they carry out their research projects. I also completed a senior honors thesis when I was an

DOI: 10.4324/9781003099406-2

undergraduate student at Occidental College in Los Angeles. I would also like to introduce my co-author, Lindsay Mitchell, who is currently working on her master's degree in neuroscience. Lindsay was a student of mine at Citrus College and later earned her bachelor's degree at California State University, Fullerton. She specializes in research, statistics, and neuroscience.

Benefits of Writing a Senior Honors Thesis

So, the first question that you are probably asking yourself is, "What are the benefits to completing a senior honors thesis?" The first and most important reason why you should consider this option during your undergraduate career is that you will be given the opportunity to gain valuable, independent research experience that might even lead you to get your research published before graduating. This will help you get into graduate school, if that is where you are headed next, or even get a job right out of college. As you conduct this project, you will have the unique opportunity to enhance your researching and data analysis skills beyond what you have learned in your basic research methods courses. This extra training will prove to be very helpful when you apply to graduate school. In fact, graduate schools and research-based jobs will want to see that you are an experienced and competent researcher, and having this type of work on your resume can make all the difference.

At this point most of your peers have only completed a research project in their introductory research methods course and might have some experience working in on-campus laboratory groups. Completing an independent honors thesis will give you a step up as you compete with these same peers for positions, either in the workforce or in professional graduate school. When you complete the requirements of the senior undergraduate honors thesis to receive departmental honors, you will receive an honors notation on your diploma and your transcript. This notation can also go on your resume and your graduate school applications.

There are many skills that you will learn and fine-tune as you work on your senior thesis project, including independent problem solving, teamwork, ethics, recruiting participants, research methodology, data analysis, and more. Although each of these skills are important, the *most important* skill you will acquire from this project is building a strong and possibly lifelong relationship with your mentor. Nothing may be more valuable to your future career than this relationship.

Let me discuss this topic in greater depth. All too often, I have seen that some undergraduate students are very focused on short-term goals, such as getting an A, finishing a project, and, even in this case, getting an honors notation. In my view, the most important thing to be concerned with, and what will get you into graduate school or help you land a job, is a strong relationship with a well-established faculty member in the field. If you build this kind of relationship with your mentor, you can lean on and utilize it for the rest of your life. As an example, my co-author Lindsay did just that. I have not only written letters on her behalf for college, graduate school, and jobs, but I also invited her to write two books with me. Those types of powerful relationships could be your ticket to a future of many successes.

Where Do I Start?

The first and most important recommendation I can give you is to *start early*. You should start thinking about completing an honors thesis at the beginning of your junior year. *Why so early?* Although it is a senior thesis, many requirements need to be completed in your junior year. If you miss those, you may not be able to graduate with honors. The first thing that you need to do is to visit your college's psychology department website and look at their information page on writing a senior honors thesis in psychology.

The first question that you might have is: "What is a senior honors thesis?" That tends to vary depending on the college or university you attend. It might be an original research project conducted largely by yourself, with the help of a mentor. It could also be a meta-analysis, a replication, and sometimes it might be part of a larger group project that has already begun. Regardless of what type of thesis you complete, you will most likely be required to design a study, collect data, analyze that data, and write up an APA experimental paper. You may also be required to present your results in either a paper or poster presentation. The bottom line is that you should do this project only if you are passionate about psychology as a science. If you are not excited about science and research, you should direct your attention elsewhere.

What Is Due During the Junior Year?

At some schools, the entire thesis takes place during the senior year. But at other colleges, the thesis is a larger project that takes place over the span of two years. Be sure to consult your school's psychology department for finer details. You might also need to enroll in a junior-year thesis course, join a lab, create a topic, write a proposal, and submit it to the Institutional Review Board (IRB). You might also have to submit an application to the department, submit progress reports to your advisor or the department, and start your experiment. At other institutions, all of the requirements take place solely during your senior year. All you need to do during your junior year is to sign up for a senior thesis course in your department.

The bottom line is that writing a senior honors thesis at your undergraduate college should be similar to the research projects that career academics conduct on a regular basis. Your project will most likely be of a much smaller scale than theirs, but you still have to go through all of the steps. The key difference is that you will have a lot the guidance from an experienced researcher.

Steps to Complete the Project

The steps that are required to complete your thesis will vary depending on the college you attend. The order of the tasks as well as timelines will also vary.

Please consult your psychology department and website for details on steps and timelines. In general, the tasks you will need to complete will look something like this:

- *Notify the department that you would like to graduate with departmental honors.* They will show you the requirements for this goal, which will include writing a thesis. You will also most likely need to fill out some paperwork for the department.
- *Register for the Senior Honors Thesis course* (it will probably have a different name).
- *Be sure to fulfill any other requirements for departmental honors.* This might include taking a test, maintaining a certain GPA, and completing assignments additional to the thesis.
- *Pick an advisor/mentor.* Some colleges will instead require you to choose a small committee and/or join a lab or research group.
- *Choose a topic and make sure your advisor can support you on that topic.* That not only means that the topic is realistic and ethical, but one in which your advisor has extensive knowledge and may help you with along the way.
- Check to see what level of review or approval your project requires from the *Institutional Review Board (IRB).*
- *Write a literature review and a methods section.* See the chapters in this book for assistance.
- *Create a proposal for the IRB.*
- *Carry out your experiment.*
- *Analyze your data and write a results and discussion section.*
- *Submit the entire paper to your advisor and/or committee for approval.*
- *Present your paper at a college event or psychology conference.*
- *Graduate with honors!*

With this introduction to the senior thesis now complete, our next step is to focus on finding a faculty mentor that has a deep knowledge of the current research related to your topic. Depending on your college, you might have just one faculty mentor or an entire committee comprised of both faculty members and graduate students. However, your psychology department will guide you on that matter and help get you started.

2 Choosing and Working With Your Mentor

Hopefully this introduction to your senior thesis has provided you with a better idea of the task ahead. It's now time for you to make your first decision, which may possibly be the most important one. It's now time to choose a mentor to help you through your project. Depending on your institution, you might need only one mentor. You may, however, need a small team of them. Typically, if you have more than one mentor, most of your time will be spent with one of them, who can be labeled as your "main mentor." You will see the others only when you need someone to read through drafts of your paper write-up.

Choosing mentors may be your most significant task in the entire senior thesis process. The good news is that you probably already have an idea of who these mentors could be. You have probably also taken classes with and had the opportunity to meet many professors at your institution. The question is, who do you want to choose to work with, day in and day out, until you complete this task?

DOI: 10.4324/9781003099406-3

In my opinion, the most important qualities that you should look for in your mentors are that they are people you get along with and they are people you can trust and rely on. You also need at least one person who really knows the topic you intend to study. If you need only one mentor and you work in a lab group, the professor who is running the lab might be an easy mentor choice. However, this decision is usually a bit more complex than that.

A mentorship Is a long-term relationship similar to the relationships you have with your family and friends. You will spend a lot of time with this person and will have to be able to agree on some things while also disagreeing about others. You will need to have good communication with this person, feel comfortable around them, respect their knowledge and abilities, and you must also be able to stand up to this person and know when it is time to back down and just listen. Does this sound familiar? You have probably encountered relationships like this before, whether it was with a sibling or parent, or even with a romantic partner. The bottom line is that this relationship is one you may want to keep for the rest of your life, and that means it will require the same kind of devotion and care you put into your personal relationships.

Mentorships, however, are a bit different from your personal relationships in some ways. First, your mentor carries some power and authority over you during your senior thesis project, as they can decide whether or not you actually graduate with honors. Second, they also have a lot more knowledge and experience than you do in the field. They will most likely be older than you and will implicitly demand a base level of respect. How you deal with this person through your project will be an important determinant of how well your project turns out. Your study may end up problematic, but if you share a good relationship with your mentor and they can advocate for how hard you have worked and how much potential you have, you are more likely to succeed in getting the honors endorsement on your degree.

Once you pick a mentor and have to begin forming that relationship with them, you may find that you are unsure how to navigate the beginnings of this type of relationship. Here are some tips I can share with you that may help you establish and maintain a good professional relationship with your new mentor. First, always show deference and respect to this person. You may not like or agree with everything they tell you, but remember that their knowledge is meant to guide you through your senior thesis journey. It is OK to question what they say, but it is important to hold some trust in what advice they give you. If you find you disagree with something they say, bring it to them and ask questions to help yourself understand where their thought process is coming from.

Second, be sure to come prepared to meetings with your mentor. Never make excuses on why you couldn't make the deadlines. Treat this like a job; if you don't meet your deadlines, you may lose that job. Your senior thesis is probably the most important thing you will do in your final year(s) of college, so it must maintain a higher level of priority.

Third, always tell your mentor the truth. Your mentor is human and therefore will have some level of understanding when things come up and cause disruption with your original project plans. If you are able to meet the goals each week that you and your mentor agree on, and you carry yourself with a level of dependability, it may be alright to not meet a goal once in a rare while. For example, if you have a family emergency and need to leave the area, just email your mentor, tell them what is happening, and communicate when you will be able to get back on track. Life happens for everyone. Just be honest, and your mentor will also be honest with you.

Also, when your study runs into some problems (and it most likely will), be sure to think about some possible solutions before you meet with your mentor. For instance, let's say you cannot gain access to the target population that you initially wanted to work with. Be sure to tell your mentor what went wrong and whether or not it can be fixed, and provide ideas on other participant populations you may want to try to recruit. Any mentor will have respect for your preparedness and "hustle" to find solutions.

My last piece of advice is to set up a routine meeting time with your mentor. There might be weeks where you don't have anything new to present. If that is the case, just email your mentor and tell them that things are coming along but you have nothing new to present this week. Be sure to ask your mentor, though, if they still want to meet with you, as they may want to discuss your progress or something else regarding your project.

Unless your mentor requests otherwise, try to make as much of your communication with them in person. We live in a high-tech world where so much of our interpersonal business is conducted through emails, texts, and DMs. It's OK to use these communication devices when needed, but nothing can exceed the benefits of a good, old-fashioned, face-to-face meeting.

Once you have established a good working relationship with your mentor, it is great to begin asking them for letters of recommendation for graduate school, for scholarships, and even for jobs. Most likely they will enjoy writing reference letters for you and being able to share with others their pride in your work. An important rule to follow when asking your professor for a letter of reference is to give them at least *two weeks* to write that letter. They may not need that much time to write it; however, it displays a level of respect for their time personal schedule. If you ask them to write a letter at the last minute, it may not only result in their saying no, but it could also change the way they think about you and your professionalism.

Question: What if your mentor invites you to their home or to a party? That can be a tough one. The reality is that you will be spending a lot of time with this person. If they live close to campus, they may ask you to meet at their house. They might even invite you to a meeting or party where there are other academics in your field. The bottom line on this topic is that you need to trust your gut. You really need to find someone that you are comfortable with. You will probably get to know their family, if they have one. If you do not feel comfortable meeting at their home, it is perfect respectable to ask if you can make all meetings on campus in a classroom or office. What is most important is that your relationship remains respectful and professional, and if you ever feel as though a situation might blur the line between a professional and more personal relationship, make decisions to guide it back in the right direction.

3   Difficult Concepts Made Easier

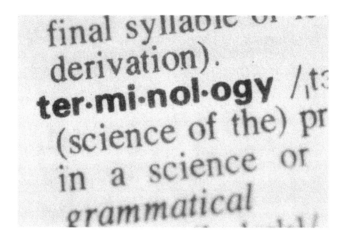

Research has a language of its own. You learned this language when you took your research methods class(es). However, if you haven't done much research lately, some of these terms may have slipped from the forefront of your mind.

This chapter has listed some of the most important concepts, and also perhaps the most challenging ones, that you will use in research. I have tried to provide you with the friendliest definitions and examples possible so you can better understand these more difficult concepts.

Alpha level: The alpha level, also called the *p*-value or (statistical) significance level, demonstrates the probability/chance of rejecting the *null hypothesis* (see the definition in this chapter) when the null hypothesis is true. In simpler words, it is the chance that you will make a wrong decision.

For example, if you test the effectiveness of a type of psychotherapy and your research study demonstrates that your psychotherapy is highly effective in reducing depression, then you have demonstrated that psychotherapy is statistically significant. However, the big question is, what are the chances that you made an error? If you used an alpha level of .05 (or 5%), that means there is a 5 percent chance that the result you received in your study occurred simply by chance (it's an error) and *not* from the psychotherapy. On a positive note, it also

DOI: 10.4324/9781003099406-4

means that there is a 95% chance that the result you received was correct and your psychotherapy did work.

Another way of looking at this is that you were to run your experiment 100 times, at least 95 or more out of 100 times that you ran the experiment, you would get the same result, showing that your treatment worked. However, with an alpha level of .05, there is a 5% chance that you will get a significant result, showing your psychotherapy was effective, even though it was *not* effective.

Many researchers feel that the 5% rule (.05) is too lenient and instead use a 1% rule (.01). If you have a strong/effective treatment, a smaller alpha level can be used to give you the confidence that your treatment really worked and removes some of the risk that you may be supplying an ineffective treatment to people that has been wrongly labeled as a good treatment.

Between-Groups Design: Also known as an *Independent Groups Design*, this is when you have an experiment that has different participants in each condition. For example, let's say you have an experiment with two conditions, one treatment group and one control group, and you are testing the effects of Prozac (treatment) against a placebo (control) on depression (the dependent variable). In this study, each of the two conditions has *different* participants – one group of participants in the treatment group, and a different group of participants in the control group.

The opposite of a Between-Groups Design is a Within-Groups Design, also called a Repeated Measures Design. In this design, one group of participants goes through *all* treatment and control conditions. Please see "Within-Groups Design" in this chapter for further details.

Confidence interval: A confidence interval is a range of scores that most likely includes the true population mean. When we state a population mean, it is never 100% accurate, as there will always be measurement error. So, if we broaden the possibilities for the mean by creating a range of scores that starts below the mean and extends to a score above the mean, it is now more likely to have the true mean contained in this range of scores.

Confidence intervals are usually stated in percentages, and a 95% confidence interval is commonly used. This means that there is only a 5% chance that our population mean does *not* fall into that range of scores. For example, if we originally state our population mean to be 20 and we say that the 95% confidence interval is from 17 to 23, that means there is only a 5% chance that our population mean does *not* fall between 17 and 23. It is a more accurate measure of a mean than using only a single score.

Confounding variable: Confounding variables are factors outside of the variables accounted for in a study that could influence the independent or dependent variables. For example, if you are conducting a study on how exercise improves memory, exercise would be the independent variable and memory would be the dependent variable. However, the type of job a person has could be a confounding variable if some of the participants in your study have more physical jobs than others, because they get more exercise. The amount of physical exercise that some participants get could influence both the IV and the

DV in your study and thus would be considered a confounding variable. If identified, a confounding variable should be controlled or eliminated. Reading journal articles on your topic can often help you identify confounding variables before you even start your study.

Construct validity: Construct validity is the ability for a test to measure what it claims to be measuring. A construct can be any sort of skill, mental quality, or ability (such as anxiety, intelligence, or depression). For example, if you create a test that measures depression, you need to show that the test you created has construct validity. The best way to do that is to give your test to a group of people and then give that same group of people other well-validated tests of depression. If your test scores correlate with the other well-validated tests, then your test has construct validity.

Content validity: Content validity is present if you have a test that measures all aspects of the domain that it is supposed to measure. For example, many concepts, such as depression or intelligence, have multiple components to them. Depression has an affective component (e.g., feeling sad), a physical component (feelings of tension, or pain), a cognitive component (thoughts of helplessness or suicide), and a behavioral component (crying). So, a test of depression would have content validity if it measured all four of these components of depression. However, if your test measured only the cognitive aspect of depression, it would lack content validity.

Correlation coefficient: A correlation coefficient is a statistic that measures the strength of the relationship between two (or more) sets of scores. A correlation tells you how closely related or unrelated those scores are. For example, two sets of scores are highly related if, given one set of numbers, you can accurately predict the other set of numbers. For example, there is some relationship between height and weight, so if you are given a person's height, you have a general idea about what their weight may be. However, since there is no relationship between age and IQ, just knowing a person's age, does *not* allow you to predict their IQ.

Correlation coefficients range between -1 and $+1$, with a 0 in the middle. If you have a correlation coefficient of $+1.0$, you have a perfect positive correlation. That means that for every score in one group that increases one unit, every score in the other variable also increases one unit. If you have a perfect positive correlation, given one set of scores, you can perfectly predict the other set of scores. The same is true for a correlation of -1.0. In a perfect negative correlation, for every unit one variable increases, the other variable *decreases* by one unit. Whether your correlation is a perfect positive or perfect negative, you always have perfect prediction. However, when you are studying people, you never get a perfect correlation because people's behavior constantly changes. The closer you are to a correlation of zero, the less of a relationship that exists between the two variables. Two variables correlated at zero have no relationship to each other, so given one variable you cannot predict the other variable at all.

Criterion validity: Criterion validity occurs if a group that scores well on a test can also perform some highly related hands-on task (criterion). For example, if a pilot enters a flight simulator and passes the simulation, the simulation has criterion validity if that pilot can now successfully fly an actual airplane. However, if a person takes a driving test at the DMV but is not able to successfully drive a car, the DMV driving test does *not* have criterion validity.

Curvilinear relationship: Many of the statistical relationships that we work with in psychology are linear relationships. That means if you were to plot out one variable on the x-axis of a graph and the other variable on the y-axis of a graph, if you connect the two scores, they will form a straight line. For example, a linear relationship exists between height and weight. As height continuously increases, weight also continuously increases. If you were to plot out people's heights and weights and connect the dots, you would get a straight line.

However, not all relationships are that simple. For some sets of variables, as one variable increases, the other variable increases at first and then decreases after that. That is a curvilinear relationship, the idea being that the two variables do not simply increase or decrease together; they have a more complicated relationship. There are several possibilities for a curvilinear relationship as seen in Graphs A, B, and C.

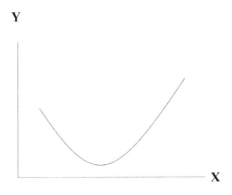

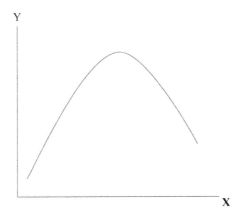

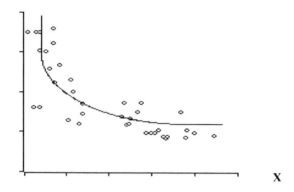

X

Degrees of freedom: The number of scores in a distribution that are free to change/vary while still maintaining the mean of the group. So, if you have ten scores in a sample, you can change nine of those ten scores (9 degrees of freedom) yet still maintain the same mean for that group. Degrees of freedom for many statistics is N − 1 or the total number of scores in that sample − one score. If there are ten scores in a sample, there are usually nine degrees of freedom.

Dependent variable: See "Independent variable" in this chapter for information on dependent variables.

Experimental method: The experimental method is a scientific approach where the researcher controls one or more independent variables and eliminates all other extraneous variables (by using random assignment and other techniques for controlling variables) to see if the dependent variable (outcome) is influenced or changed by the independent variables.

External validity: External validity is synonymous with generalizability. An experiment has external validity if the results of the study apply to a larger population. For example, a lot of research in the late 20th century did not have external validity because it was conducted on white, male college students. If your experiment's sample does not represent the population you want the results to apply to, then you do not have external validity. External validity is achieved by using a sample that resembles the larger population that you want your results to apply.

Extraneous variables: Extraneous variables are variables that are present in the study but have not been measured, and thus they might affect the outcome of the study. For example, if you were conducting a study to see if a man's height is related to his perceived attractiveness, the man's height would be the independent variable and his perceived attractiveness would be the dependent variable. However, what if, when this experiment was conducted, some rooms had walls that were painted red and other rooms had walls that were painted white? It is possible that the color of the walls might affect the way the observers feel and hence raise or lower the man's attractiveness score. In this case, the color of the walls would be the extraneous variable because it is present in the experiment but is not being measured or controlled. Extraneous variables should be removed or controlled when identified.

Face validity: Face validity is the extent to which a test *looks* or appears like it measures a construct, but it does not necessarily actually measure that construct. It is not a good measure of validity. For example, if a person takes a test that is supposed to measure their depression level and the questions appear to be measuring their depression level, then the test has face validity. Face validity alone does not prove that the test measures depression level until the test is compared to other tests of depression. It your test correlates with other tests of depression, then it has construct validity, which is a more powerful type of validity.

Independent variables and dependent variables (including experimental and control groups, as well as participant variables): In an experiment, there are two main types of variables, independent variables (IVs) and dependent variables (DVs). In short, IVs are the treatment and the variables that are to be manipulated or controlled. The DV is the outcome, result, or effect from the IV/treatment. So, if you are conducting an experiment on how Prozac affects depression, Prozac is the IV (the treatment) and depression is the DV (the outcome or effect).

The term independent variable is used only for an experiment (and not a correlation). An independent variable, by definition, must be manipulated or controlled by the experimenter. What does that mean? It means that the experimenter (the person running the experiment) must have complete control over every aspect of the IV. That means that he or she can set the strength of the IV, the length of time the IV is given, what the IV is composed of, and any other characteristic of the IV. When you can't manipulate the IV, you typically switch over to a correlation.

One example of an independent variable is a textbook. If you are trying to see if a new textbook helps kids learn more math, the textbook is the IV and math is the DV. The textbook can be manipulated by the experimenter, as the experimenter can decide what information goes into the textbook, how long the textbook is, what color the cover is., how much time the kids get to read it, and other factors.

Sometimes a variable looks like an IV but cannot be manipulated. Researchers call this a participant variable (PV). A participant variable is defined as a quality of an individual that cannot be (physically or ethically) manipulated. An example of a PV is a person's age, since age cannot be manipulated, controlled, or changed. For this reason, age is a PV and not an IV.

Another important fact about independent variables is that they must have a minimum of two groups (sometimes called conditions). Researchers call these groups experimental and control groups. The experimental group is the group that gets the treatment. For example, if you are testing the effects of Prozac on depression, the experimental group gets the Prozac.

The control group, also known as the comparison group, does *not* get the treatment. Sometimes members of the control group get nothing at all, sometimes they get a placebo, and sometimes they get the actual treatment, after the experiment is over.

At the end of the experiment, the researcher looks at how the experimental group compared to the control group influenced the dependent variable. Ideally, the experimental group had a more significant effect on the dependent variable than did the control group.

As a final note, dependent variables, which are the outcome or effect of the independent variables, are measured, not manipulated. The experiment is never allowed to alter or manipulate the DV. They simply measure it. So, if you were testing the effects of Prozac on depression. You manipulate the IV, but simply measure the level of the participant's depression.

Interaction: A statistical interaction is one of the most challenging concepts that you learned in your statistics and research methods class. An interaction can occur when you use a factorial design which is commonly analyzed using a two-way ANOVA (analysis of variance) statistic.

Here is a more detailed explanation. A factorial design means that your study has more than one independent variable. For example, if you are conducting a study on how Prozac and psychotherapy affect depression levels, you have two independent variables (Prozac and Psychotherapy) and one dependent variable (depression). This is a factorial design. When you run an ANOVA on your data you will get two different types of results, *main* effects (two of them) and an *interaction*. A main effect simply means that each independent variable influences your dependent variable. For example, if Prozac reduced depression, then this study would have a significant first main effect (because Prozac is the first independent variable). If psychotherapy also reduced depression scores, then this study would have a second main effect (main effect of the second variable, psychotherapy). So main effects simply mean that each independent variable has a statistically significant effect on the dependent variable.

What about the interaction? An interaction is when the two factors (independent variables) work together (in conjunction with each other) to affect the DV of depression. For example, when we look at the main effects of this study, we see that Prozac reduces depression and psychotherapy reduces depression. So, if you gave some of the participants in your study both Prozac and psychotherapy, you would expect them to have even less depression than if you were just to give them one of the treatments. So far, we are seeing just the two main effects, and not an interaction.

An interaction is when the two treatments work together to create some *unusual* or *atypical* result. So, if you were to give participants in this study both treatments, Prozac and Psychotherapy, and they were to experience *more* (rather than less) depression, that would be an interaction. It would also be an interaction if both treatments made participants physically ill, since that is not an effect of either treatment on its own.

The best and easiest way to detect an interaction is to look at the graphs from the ANOVA. Most statistical software programs such as SPSS should make these graphs for you. If in your graph the two lines for the main effects *cross* each other, then you have an interaction. If the two lines are parallel to each other or do *not* cross, there is no interaction. In the graphs below Graph A has no interaction, but Graph B has an interaction.

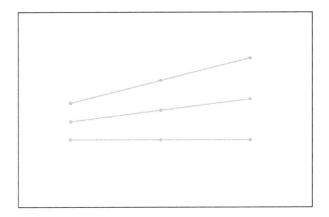

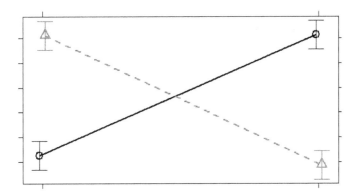

Internal validity: Internal validity is another word for causation. Internal validity in an experiment means that the independent variable is the only variable that caused a change in the dependent variable. If a study has high internal validity, there are no extraneous or confounding variables in the study and hence *all* influences/changes to the dependent variable were caused by the independent variable and nothing else. Internal validity is an extremely important part of an experiment.

Matched Pairs Design: A Matched Pairs Design is an experimental design that typically uses a participant variable (PV; see "Independent variables" in this chapter for more information on participant variables) such as age or gender. When PVs are used, randomization becomes unavailable because you cannot manipulate the participant variable. As a result, you need to find two sets of participants that are equally matched on that key PV such as IQ. Simply put, for every person in group A with a certain IQ score, there must be a person in group B with that same IQ score.

Measurement scales (nominal, ordinal, interval, ratio): Measurement scales are the ways in which variables/numbers are categorized and defined. There are four different scales of measurement, from lowest to highest; they are nominal, ordinal, interval, and ratio. *Nominal scale* simply means that the data or numbers you have only *name* the variable; they don't tell you anything about the quality of the data. For example, I could name three brands of cars, Ford, Chevy, and Toyota. Types of cars are Nominal data because they are just names and don't denote which one is better, worse, higher, or lower than the others. Another example of nominal scale data is the category colors; red, blue, white. Colors are nominal because red, blue, and white are just labels and don't denote which is higher or lower, or better or worse, than the others.

Nominal data, like most kinds of data, can also be numbers, if the numbers do *not* demonstrate quality, such as better or worse or higher or lower. For example, numbers on a football jersey are nominal, because although the number 52 is higher than 12, these numbers just identify a specific player and *not* whether that player is better or worse than the other players. Other examples of nominal scale data include people's names, race, ethnicity, or the style of house they live in (e.g., ranch vs. colonial).

Ordinal scale data is the least-used type of data. Ordinal refers to *rank order* data, such as who finished the race in first, second, or third place. Unlike nominal data, ordinal scale data does tell you whether the person did better or worse. Higher numbers denote a better or worse score. For example, first place is better than second place, and second place is better than third place.

So, unlike nominal scale data, the number is more than a label; it denotes who did better or worse. The weakness with ordinal data is that there are not equal distances between data points. For example, John finished the race in *first* place with a time of 35 seconds. Mike finished the race in *second* place with a time of 38 seconds. David finished the race in *third* place with a time of 128 seconds. So, although first place is better than second place, and second place is better than third place, the time difference between first and second place (38–35 seconds = 3 seconds) is not the same difference as that between second place and third place (128 seconds − 38 seconds = 90 seconds). So, the first- and second-place runners were close in time (3 seconds' difference), but third place was far behind second place (90 seconds' difference).

Interval scale data is more useful and powerful in an experiment than nominal or ordinal scale data. With interval scale data, higher numbers are better or worse than lower numbers. For example, a temperature of 104 degrees is worse than a temperature of 99 degrees, and an IQ of 140 is better than an IQ of 97. The other quality of interval scale data is that there are *equal intervals* between each number. For example, using a Fahrenheit thermometer, the difference between 98 and 99 degrees is the same as the difference between 101 and 102 degrees. So, with interval scale data, higher is better, or worse, and there are equal intervals between each number on the scale. The final aspect of an interval scale is that there is *no* absolute zero. Simply put, in an interval scale, scores either don't go all the way down to zero, or they go below zero, but they do *not* completely stop at zero. Your professor may recommend that the dependent variable in your experiment be interval or ratio scale.

The final type of measurement scale is called ratio. Ratio is very similar to interval, with one big difference. Like interval data, ratio data demonstrates that higher numbers are better or worse than lower numbers, and there are also equal intervals between each number on the scale. The one difference with ratio data is that it has an absolute zero. An absolute zero means that when you reach zero on that scale, you have a complete absence of that quality. For example, zero pounds is a complete absence of weight. You cannot weigh less than zero pounds. A ratio scale must go all the way down to zero but can never go below it. There are *no* negative scores in ratio data. Examples of ratio data are height (inches or meters), weight (pounds or grams), or volume (ounces or milligrams). With ratio data, you can also make ratios. For example, 100 pounds is twice as heavy at 50 pounds and 6 feet is twice as tall as 3 feet. You cannot do that with an interval scale.

Null hypothesis: A hypothesis stating that the mean of the control group is equivalent to the mean of your treatment group. If the null hypothesis is true, then your treatment had no effect on your sample. If you reject the null hypothesis, you are saying that your treatment was effective and the treatment group mean is greater (or less) than the mean of the control group.

Quasi experiment: A quasi-experiment is similar to a true experiment except you do *not* use random assignment (please see the "Random assignment" description that follows). If you can manipulate an independent variable, you can typically use random assignment and create a true experiment. However, if you are using a participant variable (please see the description of independent variables in this chapter) that cannot be manipulated than you cannot use random assignment. Without random assignment, you have a quasi-experiment (meaning not quite an experiment). For example, if you are interested in whether men vs. women do better on a math test, you cannot manipulate gender, and thus you cannot use random assignment. Because you are using a PV and not an IV, you have a quasi-experiment.

Random assignment: Random assignment is when every participant in your study has an equal chance of being placed in the experimental or control group. For example, if you have a population of 100 participants and you want half of the participants to be in the experimental group and the other half to be in the control group, you would generally use random assignment. To create random assignment, you could use a computer to assign every participant a number, for example, and then place the odd-numbered participants into the experimental group and the even-numbered participants into the control group. Random assignment is one of the most important qualities of a true experiment and a technique that helps reduce extraneous variables.

Type I error. A type I error, also known as a false positive, is when a person rejects the null hypothesis when it should have been accepted. In other words, it occurs when you test a treatment's effectiveness and your experiment shows that the treatment is effective, yet had your study been done correctly, it would have shown that the treatment did not work. Since your experiment showed that the treatment was effective, you sell a useless treatment to lots of people.

Type II error. A type II treatment, or a false negative, is when you accept the null hypothesis and say that your treatment did not work, but really your treatment was effective and it *did* work. In a sense, you are throwing out good treatments and knowledge. For example, let us say that you test to see if a new textbook is better for learning than an old textbook. If the new books *are* better than the old book, but your research shows that the books are essentially the same, than you have committed a type II error. Type II errors usually occur when you have a smaller sample size or your treatment is effective but not overly strong.

Within-Groups Design (also known as a Repeated Measures Design): In a Within-Groups Design, the *same* group of participants experiences all conditions, both treatment and control. For example, if you have two conditions, one control/placebo group and one treatment group, one group of participants would first receive the placebo for a period of time and then the *same* group of participants would receive the treatment for a period of time. Each participant would act as their own control by receiving both the control condition and the treatment condition. When the experiment was complete, the researcher would look at the scores from both treatment and control conditions to see if the treatment had a different effect on the participants than the control/placebo.

The Within-Groups Design is a preferred technique for two reasons: It uses far fewer participants compared to the Between-Groups Design, and it has a lot less statistical error. Less error increases your chances of rejecting the null hypothesis and getting a statistically significant (successful) result from your treatment.

The main challenge of the Within-Groups Design is that it cannot be used if your treatment has carryover effects. Carryover effects is when your treatment has a long lasting or even permanent effect on your participants. If you have carryover effects, you must avoid the Within-Groups Design and use a Between-Groups Design.

The Within-Groups Design can be used only in experiments where the treatment is short-lived. When using the Within-Groups Design, you must also use Counterbalancing (also known as a Latin Square) to help remove order effects. Please see a research methods textbook for more information on Counterbalancing, Order Effects, and Latin Squares.

Part II

Designing Your Experiment and Writing Your Proposal

4 Picking a Topic and Designing Your Experiment

Designing your experiment is the first "hands-on" step in your senior thesis project. Even though you may be designing it by yourself, be sure to work closely with your mentor to make sure your methodology is accurate. If your study has a poor design and you try to run subjects or analyze the data, it may not work. The first two steps in this process are, first, to decide what your hypotheses will be and, second, what type of research study you will conduct to test your hypotheses (e.g., survey, observation, experiment, etc.). The type of research study that you do may be decided by your school's guidelines, but choosing the topic will be largely up to you.

Before Beginning Your Project

Before you start your research project, you should check any guidelines or documents that your college has provided for you. Chances are that your mentor

DOI: 10.4324/9781003099406-6

has some idea of what he or she wants to see in your project. When it comes to deciding what type of research study you want to do, there are different types to choose from: archival data, observations, survey projects, and experiments. It is important to make sure that your college will allow you to do the type of study that you are interested in before you begin. If you choose to start collecting data before gaining approval from your college, you may be asked to redesign your entire study due to methodological or ethical issues.

Ethical Considerations

Regardless of the type of research study that you decide to execute, it must follow ethical guidelines outlined by the American Psychological Association (APA). Studies you might see today that are deemed unethical do not look the same as some of the ones you remember learning about in Psychology 101 that included shocking people or locking them up in a mock-jail setting and leaving them to behave as they wished. Even the most harmless of studies can be carried out unethically if all aspects of the process are not accounted for and thoroughly monitored. This is why you should always run your ideas by your mentor before carrying them out. Their experience running research studies allows them to see possible ethical gaps in your study before they become problematic.

Most mentors will advocate more for a research idea that is not too controversial. Quite often a student will want to perform an exciting project that they think could lead to some groundbreaking results. Although these types of projects are valuable, they are better left for professional researchers who have the means to conduct the study properly with the ability to find viable and generalizable results. Remember that the purpose of this project is for you to learn and display your knowledge on how to perform a research study independently. Although you may aspire to become one of the world's leading researchers one day, you must first be allowed to learn the process and make mistakes along the way with a smaller-scale study.

In the past, I have had students who requested study topics that involved inducing stress or using coercive techniques to find answers to their hypotheses, often because the student had learned about these types of studies in their psychology classes. Keep in mind that the APA ethics code is currently much stricter than it used to be, and many studies that you might have read about in your introductory psychology classes have now been banned. So, before you start your research study, ask yourself this: *Would you and your family members agree to be participants in the study exactly the way it is designed?* If your answer is no, it's time to come up with a new approach. Remember, neither you nor your school wants to be put in a sticky legal situation, so be sure to consult your mentor and gain approval before interacting with participants.

Possible Topics

With so many ethical guidelines to follow, what are some possible research topics that can be done in a short amount of time, and that don't create too much controversy? Good news: There are journals full of clean yet fun topics out there that you can explore for your study. For example, you could provide an intervention to improve individuals' short-term memory recall. You could also visit a workplace and offer an intervention to improve productivity or increase employee happiness. Sometimes you can even employ a confederate to act in a certain manner and see what the results are. For instance, you could have someone sit on a public park bench, a little too close to a stranger, and see how the stranger reacts.

If you are working with a group in a specific lab, your project may already be clearly defined if your group has already completed several studies on a given topic. You can either add in a new variable to the study or piggyback off a larger study. If your mentor likes the idea, you can run with it. Either way, you will want to base your research project on information that has already been found in previous studies. Just be sure to always use peer-reviewed scholarly journal articles. For further information on the APA ethical guidelines for human and animal research, please check out the apa.org website.

Decisions, Decisions . . .

Once you have some basic ideas for your hypothesis and design, you need to make a few decisions. Are you going to work with humans, or with animals? Will you work in a laboratory or a classroom, or will you collect data out in the field? Can you do your study online? Must it be an experiment, or can it be an archival study, observation, or survey? How much time do you have to carry out the study? These are all integral questions that you must be able to answer to properly plan out your project. You might have only a couple of weeks to run your study from start to finish, or you might have months to complete it, so plan carefully and make sure that the project doesn't become too large for your given deadlines. *Time* is a very important variable in your study. *Budget* is also very important. You might be paying for all of your supplies out of your own pocket, or the college might be paying for them. Your mentor should give you guidance on all of these questions, but if they have not already done so, be sure to ask these questions before getting too far into an idea.

As I mentioned at the start of this chapter, many senior thesis mentors require their students to conduct experiments rather than correlational studies. This is because an experiment is a much more complex project compared to an associative study. Most undergraduate psychology students have a pretty good grasp of what is required for an experiment. However, since it might have been a year or two since your research methods class, here is a quick review.

For a research study to be an experiment, it must have two elements: (1) an independent variable that is completely manipulated and controlled by the researcher, and (2) the experiment must use random assignment. Let's first consider what a manipulable independent variable looks like.

A true independent variable is one that the researcher can create, change, or modify in any way that they want. For example, if a researcher is testing out a new book in the classroom, the new book can be created or manipulated to reflect what the researcher is trying to accomplish. The researcher controls what pages or pieces of information go into that book, how long the book is, which students or classes get the book, what color the book is, and anything else that they deem important. Another example of a variable that can be manipulated is a new medication. The researcher determines how much medication the participants get, how many participants get the medication, how many do not get it, and so on.

Independent variables are often treatments or interventions such as Cognitive Behavioral Therapy (CBT) or an Anger Management Training. For each of these variables, the researcher can manipulate what these therapy sessions will look like by controlling their content and length as well as the type of therapy used. Because the researcher can manipulate them in these ways, it shows that they are true independent variables.

In contrast, let's take a quick look at variables that *cannot* be manipulated and hence *cannot* be an independent variable in an experiment. For example, you cannot manipulate or change a person's age or ethnicity. There are additional variables that can be physically changed, but it is considered unethical to do so. Self-esteem would be an example of this type of variable. It is possible to lower a person's self-esteem, but it is generally considered to be unethical because it can cause severe damage to mental health. Variables that cannot be manipulated physically or ethically cannot be independent variables in an experiment. They can, however, be used in other types of experiments like correlations and quasi-experiments.

The first test to see if you can run a true experiment is to make sure that you have at least one variable that you can control completely. Be sure to think about how many independent, dependent, and confounding variables you have the time and resources to examine. You may really want to work with your mentor on this because adding a variable can change everything from the time and energy that is required for the project to your statistical analysis. It can also make your project more complicated, sometimes steering it outside your abilities. In my opinion, you don't want to have more than two independent variables and one dependent variable per experiment. You may also want to limit the number of confounding variables you examine to two or three. Even though you are running a full-scale experiment that you might intend to publish, you want to keep the depth of your study reasonable.

A second way to test your independent variable would be to see if you can implement random assignment with all of your participants. Random assignment requires that every participant in your study have an equal chance of falling into any of the possible groups (such as *experimental* and *control* groups).

Imagine that you are running an experiment and you have brought 100 participants into the room. Your plan is to assign 50 people to the experimental group and the remaining 50 in the control group. To do this, you must randomly assign each of those individuals a unique number. You can accomplish this by having them each draw a number out of a hat, or even by using a randomized number generator. Then you must have a method of equally splitting them into each respective group. For instance, you could place every participant who is assigned an odd number into group 1 (the experimental group), while those given an even number will be placed in group 2 (the control group).

Now that you have created your groups using random assignment, it's time to introduce your independent variable to your participants. Remember that the independent variable is something that you introduce to the participants *from the outside*. It cannot already be something that the participants are exposed to, and it should be introduced only to those in the experimental group. In short, if the variable can be manipulated, you have an experiment. If the variable cannot be manipulated, you have a quasi-experiment or a correlation. As always, be sure to clear your design and variables with your mentor before moving forward with participant interactions.

Additional Thoughts

One thing I like to always tell my research students is that they need to remain open to change because things do not always go according to plan. Let's say you have already planned out your research study, but suddenly you are told that you can no longer run it at the location you had set up. This can create quite a wave for you and the course of your project, but remember that it is not the only location out there that can work for you. Begin focusing your attention on looking elsewhere and alter your plans accordingly. Even the greatest of planning does not guarantee that you will be successful in carrying out your study exactly the way you first envisioned it.

I once did a research job in a prison, and from day one the staff was trying to push me and my team out. Ask yourself this: Would you be comfortable with a reality TV show being taped in your home? Conducting a research study in someone else's workplace can create a similar feeling to the workers who are employed there, and this can cause problems for you if you decide to run your study similarly. Even conducting research in a laboratory can lead to obstacles and failures. My main advice is this: always have a plan B. Have an idea for new variables, a new setting, and even a whole new experiment. In the end, you are required to complete this project to graduate with honors, so the more flexible you are, the more likely you are to get there.

Nonexperimental Designs

I have spent a great deal of time discussing experimental designs. However, your mentor may be perfectly content with your conducting a survey or correlational study, depending on the variables that you are using. There is nothing wrong with correlational research, and in many cases it might be your only choice. In fact, most of the published research in psychology journals are correlational due to ethical limitations. The biggest difference between experimental and correlational research is that experiments are carried out in the here and now and correlations occur post hoc (after the fact). Correlations have fewer design issues and fewer ethical issues, and they use different statistics. Correlational designs also typically use multiple regression and correlation, whereas experiments more often use ANOVA, MANOVA, and t-tests.

5 Submitting a Proposal for IRB Approval

One of the most important steps in your research study, and a potential hurdle to completion, is getting approval for your project from the Institutional Review Board (IRB). The main job of the IRB is to assess the methodology of your study and monitor the potential risk of your study with regard to your subjects. They are there to protect you and your college from being sued, but also to protect the welfare of your participants.

There are a couple of things that you need to think about when you begin working with the IRB. Their big question is, "How much risk does your study pose for the participants, and is that risk necessary?" Colleges frown upon research studies that involve a lot of risk, especially if they are not outweighed by the benefits. For example, a research university testing out a new drug for cancer may allow more potential risk to a participant if there is a chance of creating a better treatment. However, a university is not going to look positively

DOI: 10.4324/9781003099406-7

on a study that causes either physical or psychological harm to a participant with little to gain except for some general knowledge.

In the end, the IRB has the ability to deny your study or ask for amendments to its design. They, of course, also have the ability to accept it the way it was submitted. Most of the time, the IRB will look at your study's proposal and ask you questions about your research methodology and/or the potential risks involved. Your answers to those questions will help them determine if your study gets approved, denied, or sent back to you with necessary alterations. There are some smaller schools and ones that focus primarily on teaching instead of research that don't have an IRB. In that instance you would defer to your faculty mentor or department chair to make decisions about the efficacy and safety of your study.

Is IRB Approval Always Required?

The quick answer to this question is that it is usually required, but not always. Because the IRB process is detailed and lengthy, when you propose a new study, the most important thing that you need to do is to discuss your study with your mentor before you put too much effort into writing a proposal. That way, you will find out if an IRB approval is needed. If approval is needed, you will have to focus on the IRB process from day one.

As previously discussed, one main focus of the IRB will be the welfare of your research participants. Many colleges now require all researchers to complete an online ethics training regarding the use of human subjects. At those schools, a researcher is unable to submit an IRB proposal until they have completed this ethics training. Some schools use a more cut-and-dried approach to determining if a study requires IRB approval by creating categories. For instance, they may automatically require a full IRB approval for high-risk projects, a smaller review for those of lesser risk, and exemptions for projects without any risk involved.

The rest of this chapter will focus on IRB documents and procedures you might be required to complete in order to gain their approval. This is not a comprehensive list of tasks, but rather some of the most common tasks required by US and UK colleges.

Application: Chances are that your college will have an application that you need to fill out even if your research project is exempt from an IRB review. You still need to explain to the college what you are researching and why it would be exempt from the full screening process. Reasons for exemption might include research that involves only anonymous surveys, or archival research. The application will also ask who the principal researchers are and any other researchers affiliated with the project. It will most likely ask for their education and current training.

Human subjects: There is always a section in the application that asks about human subjects. It will require you to describe everything that your human subjects will experience during your research project. You must include any scripts, consent forms, and debriefings that the subjects will receive. You will also need to describe the equipment that will be used during the study. If medications are used, you will be required to provide additional documentation about its safety. The IRB will be looking to see if you are in compliance with all HIPAA guidelines, so it may be useful to pre-check those guidelines ahead of time.

Subject pool and recruitment of research participants and subjects: Your college will want to know how you are recruiting the participants for your study. Are you recruiting students from on campus or off campus? Are your participants medical patients being treated in the clinic or hospital, or did they sign up for a clinical trial? *Coercion* is a big red flag that the IRB will be looking for. Did you provide incentives to recruit your participants? Were they paid money? Were they given extra credit points? Were they promised a new drug for life? Some colleges find these practices acceptable, while others do not. If you are using animals in your study, are you purchasing them from an acceptable location? How are you planning to care for them? What will be done to these animals? Colleges typically have animal rights groups watching them closely and may protest or sue the college if they feel the animals are being treated unethically.

Confidentiality and sensitive information: The college will want to know how you protected your participants' confidentiality. Confidentiality is required whether you are carrying out a simple survey or evaluating something as sensitive as health-related tests. Your college's IRB wants to know how participants are informed about the details of the study, how you handle their private information, and how you destroy confidential information at the end of the study, if this is needed. They will also want to know how you disseminate the conclusions of your research and how much information you share about the participants in your results.

Benefits and risks to participants: The college wants to know what risks the participants might face, in both the short term and long term, as well as what benefits each participant might gain by being a part of this study. Think about this scenario: A medical researcher is planning on researching a group of participants with HIV by giving them either a medication or a placebo to help reduce their symptoms. Each treatment has the potential to create further complications or long-term benefits. How will the researcher take each of these outcomes into account and balance the risks with the possible benefits?

Budget and funding: The university will want to know if you have the funds to complete this study and where any funding is coming from. You will want to avoid accepting any funding from agencies that insert bias into your study as a condition of their help. Work to keep your study as free from bias as possible.

Use of children as human participants: If you want to include children in your study, an additional set of forms will be required to show that you will receive all of the appropriate written approval from their parents or legal guardians.

Summary of the project: All applications typically ask for a summary of the entire project. It may be something as short as two or three pages, or it may require that you include your entire literature review along with a description of your intended methods. Please read the instructions carefully for this section of your school's IRB review. Every college may require something a little different.

IRB approval can be an intimidating process that involves a lot of time and energy. To be honest, you have little control over the IRB's decisions. You submit the best version of your study to researchers from different departments within your university for analysis and critique in the hopes that they will accept it and you can move forward. However, the process is rarely that simple. Be sure to start early and make your deadlines so that you can move on as soon as you can to data collection. With that information in hand, it's now time to start thinking about how you will write your experimental paper.

6 Understanding Journal Articles

As you write the Introduction and Literature Review for your senior thesis project, you will be reading a lot of journal articles. Most of these articles will come from your university library's databases, but don't forget to utilize research from places like the Interlibrary Loan (ILL) if you can't find the articles that you need. Almost all psychology journal articles are formatted in accordance with the *Publication Manual of the American Psychological Association*. As a result, you will find that almost all these articles have the same general organization and key elements. In this chapter I will discuss in detail the organization and key elements that you can find in each article.

It's important to start off here with a few tips on where to find good-quality journal articles and how to avoid any potential bad ones. You have probably heard by now that you should always use peer-reviewed journal articles. "Peer-reviewed" means that the author submits the article to a journal to be

DOI: 10.4324/9781003099406-8

published, and the journal's editor then sends the article out to a couple of reviewers. The reviewers' job is to read the article and decide if the article is suitable for printing. Their decision is based on the originality of the article as well as the quality and authenticity of the article's findings. If the reviewers decide that the article is of good quality, they recommend publication to the editor. Next, the editor must decide if the journal should publish that researcher's article. This entire process can sometimes take as long as one year before it finally becomes published.

There is now a very popular type of internet publication called *Open Access* or *OA*. Open Access includes articles that can be downloaded and shared for free. There are generally two different types of OA research: (1) archives or repositories, and (2) journals. OA archives are generally considered not quite of the same quality as OA journals because the archives are not peer-reviewed. This means that anyone can publish their work in this location. OA journals, however, are still free to the end user but are peer-reviewed during the publication process. When you conduct a database search, you should always look for peer-reviewed journal articles, whether they come from private or free databases.

Here is the big question: Just because a journal article is peer-reviewed, does that make it accurate? When you send an article to a journal to be published, the reviewers do not run your experiment again to test the results. The reviewers take your word for it, to a certain degree, that your data is accurate and valid. However, sometimes people carry out scientific research, yet still reach inaccurate results due to errors in their methodology. Other times, a researcher may blatantly fake or plagiarize their data and publish their inaccurate results.

Regardless of whether the errors came from a flawed research design or from plagiarism, the psychology community is now experiencing what is known as a replication crisis. The replication crisis is concerned with the fact that some of the most famous research ever done in psychology, as well as many lesser-known studies, are unable to be accurately replicated. In addition, many studies that are able to be replicated are not producing the same results as those by the original researcher(s). This crisis is present in both OA research and in reputable journals. As a result, the quality of many journal articles is now being called into question and retested for accuracy. So, to answer our big question, not all peer-reviewed journal articles should be seen automatically as truthful and accurate. Employ your researching skills and look out for any red flags that emerge while reading through a journal article before you cite the article in your write-up.

Now that you have a better idea of where to find good-quality journal articles, let's discuss the organization and structure of a journal article and where to find all the important parts. In your senior thesis, you will very likely be writing an APA experimental paper that is similar to the journal articles you have been exposed to already in some of your previous psychology courses. However, the formatting that you see published in journal articles may differ from the way that APA requires you to write your papers. APA tells you exactly how to format your experimental write-ups, but when a journal publishes that paper, they make several changes in the formatting so that it meets their needs and preferences. Since this chapter focuses mainly on reading and understanding journal articles, we will not spend much time on how to format your own paper. We will focus instead on what you will see when you read a published journal article. In future chapters of this book, we will discuss in greater depth how to write and format the various sections of an APA experimental paper. With that in mind, it is now time to take a close look at the key sections of a published APA experimental paper.

Title page: The title page of an APA paper has several key elements including a running head (found in the upper left-hand corner of the page), a page numbering (found in the upper right-hand corner of the page), a title, authors' names, the institution where each author works, and sometimes an author note.

A running head is a brief, summarized title that you will find in the upper left corner of a title page. Its purpose dates back to a time before computers. Back in those days, researchers would have to mail a hard copy of their paper to a publishing journal. What would happen, then, if the pages were dropped, and all manners of written works got scrambled together? The running head would help reidentify which pages went with which written work. Although a running head is not as important in the computer era, it is still required by APA to prevent this same issue from occurring.

Abstract: Although an abstract is typically the first part of the paper that you read, it is usually the final portion of the paper that is written. An abstract is an overview of 250 words or less that summarizes an experimental paper from start to finish. Sometimes an abstract is a good representation of the entire paper, while other times it is not. When you are conducting a library search for journal articles on your topic, don't be fooled by the abstract, as they are not always accurate. Be sure to also look at the full version of the journal article. After reading the actual article, you will find that the abstract either was or was not an accurate summary.

Introduction: The introduction, sometimes referred to as a *literature review* (although the literature review is actually only one portion of the full introduction section), is the first main section of your paper. In the introduction, you will encounter the following pieces of information: a statement of the problem, a literature review, and a hypothesis. The first part of this opening section is meant to catch your attention and lure you into reading the rest of the article. I like to call this section "the statement of the problem." For example, if you are conducting research on a new treatment for depression, the statement of the problem would include information such as how many people die each year as a result of severe depression, how many days of work are missed due to depressive illness, and how much money depression costs the country each year.

The largest part of the introduction section is the literature review. A literature review includes a summary of past research studies that either support or contradict the hypothesis of the paper. For example, if the hypothesis of the paper is that Cognitive Behavioral Therapy (CBT) reduces depression in middle-aged adults, the literature review will be filled with recent research that supports this conclusion. The literature review might also include broader but related topics such as the effects of CBT on depression in younger adults, or even gender differences in the use of CBT on depression. The literature review is sometimes called a "vote count," as it's a summary of both the research supporting your hypothesis as well as the research that does not support your hypothesis.

The final element of the introduction section describes the hypotheses. There could be one brief hypothesis, such as "the present study hypothesized that CBT would reduce depression in middle-age adults," or there could be multiple hypotheses. Once the hypotheses have been stated, that marks the end of the introduction. It then leads into the *methods* section. The main purpose of a methods section is to show how the experiment was conducted. It is all about details and replication; your methods portion needs to be written with so much detail that anyone reading it could rerun the study in exactly the same way that the original researchers did it. When you write your own papers, it is important to put a great amount of detail into your methods section. Let's put it this way: If it feels like you are going overboard with information, you are on the right track. If you fail to provide all necessary information, your study will not be able to be replicated and its findings will become worthless.

There are three main parts of a methods section: (1) participants, (2) materials, and (3) procedures. The *participants* component should provide information about the pool of individuals who participated in the study. For example, let's say your study included 100 participants between 18 and 22 years of age who were selected from a large midwestern public university. All of that information should be clearly stated here. There should also be information about the participants' demographic variables, such as their ethnicity, race, culture, socioeconomic status, and any other information that is relevant to the topic and may have implications on the study's results. After reading the *participants* subsection, you should have a clear understanding of who was included in the study and therefore to whom its results apply.

The second part of the methods section is the *materials* component. At this point, any information such as the study's location and any apparatuses used, such as tests, machines, computers, or software programs, should be listed. Be sure to identify these as *operational definitions*. An operational definition is a clear description of a variable or concept along with how it was measured. If a researcher is studying love, he or she should clearly define what "love" means with regards to their study as well as what test they are using to measure it. We will spend more time discussing how to write operational definitions later in this book.

The final portion of the methods section that you will write includes the study's *procedures*. The procedures section includes a step-by-step process of how the study was conducted, starting with the researcher's very first contact with each participant and ending with the participant leaving the study. Just like the other sections, the procedures section should provide an immense amount of detail that would allow any reader to run the study exactly as it was conducted in the original experiment.

The next section you will find in an APA experimental paper is the *results* section. It's fair to say that many students, and perhaps even some professionals, rarely look forward to reading the results section of a paper because it is loaded with raw statistical language. However, understanding statistics is an integral part of being a researcher. It is in the results section that the researcher truly shows if their claims are justified. For example, a researcher who runs a study on the effectiveness of a new drug for cancer treatment might find that their original hypothesis – which claimed that drug "X" successfully slows the growth of cancer cells – was correct. They are going to have to clearly show the statistic that backs up this claim so that a reader can understand exactly how effective the drug was.

There are a few key components in a results section that you will want to look out for in an article. It will, at the very least, contain a summary of the results found from any statistical tests run on the data as well as with whether or not each test was significant. A results section also typically contains visual aids such as tables and figures to help illustrate the statistical findings. Many readers enjoy these because they help portray the results of statistical tests without the need to understand statistical language.

The final key section of an APA experimental paper is the *discussion* section. It is the least structured section you will find in an experimental paper, as it allows for the researcher's interpretations of a study's results. The discussion's main goal is to make the results of a study meaningful. It should explain why the study was done, why the results are important, and how the results can be used to benefit the topic they chose. A discussion section often starts by summarizing the results of the study and explaining why the results are useful to the reader. It also typically illustrates what the limitations of the study were and provides feedback as to what went wrong while running the study. The final sentences usually explain what the researcher's next study will look like based on the findings of the current study. A good researcher will explain the statistical results from the experiment in a more reader-friendly style in their discussion. For that reason, some readers skip the results section completely and jump right to reading the discussion section, because it is simpler to understand.

After the discussion section, the only thing left to include are a study's references. Every journal article cited in the entire paper should be included in the form of a list that is labeled as *references*. You might find this list handy when you are writing your own papers on the same or a similar topic, as it is a great way to find research that supports your hypothesis.

7 Writing a Literature Review

The first major section of your senior thesis will be the introduction, including your literature review. As you already read in the chapter on understanding journal articles, the purpose of the literature review is to summarize research that both supports and challenges your hypothesis. As an example, let's say you hypothesize that listening to classical music improves explicit memory retention. This hypothesis has two variables: classical music, which is the IV; and explicit memory retention, as the DV. It's important that your hypothesis be narrow, focused, and carefully described with the correct terminology; otherwise, you may have trouble finding relevant research on the topic. If you had picked a more ambiguous topic, such as the effects of music on memory, your database search would turn up a wide array of results, many of which would not even be useful to your study. This is because "music" and "memory" have numerous subcategories, and all of them would pop up.

DOI: 10.4324/9781003099406-9

Once you have narrowed down your hypothesis, you can begin to search databases for scholarly research. A few tips about your search: First and most important, never do a Google search for articles on your topic. It also may be best to avoid open access journal articles for now, and to use them only during later searches if you run into trouble finding necessary research for your topic. A scholarly researcher, such as yourself, should always begin by searching databases of peer-reviewed scholarly psychological research. No Internet, no magazines, and no newspapers should be used. Use your college's psychology databases, and use very specific terms. You will want to refer to articles that are current, ideally within the last five to ten years. Avoid referencing older research unless it is used to introduce your topic and to lay the foundation for newer studies you will be referencing.

When students have trouble finding articles, it's usually because they don't use sufficiently focused search terms. Sometimes finding the right search terms is achieved through trial and error, and sometimes it will require the help of your mentor. If you find yourself searching term after term and not bringing up quality research on your topic, seek the help of your mentor before getting too discouraged. A lot of times, a more experienced researcher will be able to help guide you on which terms will work and which ones will not. Your mentor might also give you an idea of how many articles should be referenced in your literature review. However, remember that more is always better, granted that all of the chosen articles are relative to your topic and hypotheses. It's not uncommon to have over 40 articles for a single research paper.

When gathering research articles to use in your literature review, be sure to look through an entire article – not just the abstract – before deciding to include it in your write-up. I have witnessed many students make the mistake of gathering a stack of 40 articles that they feel are relevant for their paper based solely on the abstract. The problem is that abstracts do not always accurately represent the information found in the full article. An abstract may look great at first glance, but remember that an abstract is an extremely short summary of a study and its findings. By nature, an abstract leaves out more details than it includes. This means that you, the reader, will also be missing a large majority of a study's information by just reading the abstract.

Once you have chosen all of the articles you need to write a full literature review, the next step is to organize those articles in a sensible way. One way to organize is based on the variable it discusses. For example, you can make one pile for the articles that discuss your independent variable, another pile for those that discuss your dependent variable, and a third pile for articles that study both your independent and dependent variables. In the third pile, you might even want to divide it into two more categories: one for articles that support your hypotheses, and another for articles that contradict your hypotheses. You can also organize your articles based on the year in which they were published or simply based on the sequence of their findings. There is no right or wrong way to do this. Just do what will be helpful for you as you go through the process of piecing all of the articles together in your paper.

At some point you may find summarizing each article useful before you begin the writing process; that way you already have an idea of how to introduce and explain each article in your own words. Writing a summary of research articles is like writing an annotated bibliography. It involves reading the entire article and briefly describing it based on section (introduction, methods, results, etc.). As a general rule, don't provide a summary of more than four sentences on any given section unless it's extremely important. When you summarize an article, you can also critique it. For example, if you find an article that supports your hypothesis, it is also important to point out any of the article's flaws. A good researcher will state when a supportive article has too small of a sample size or didn't randomize their participants properly. Later, when you create your own experiment, you can identify how your study will address these same problems you found in previous studies.

One of the most common issues found in student writing that I should address here is plagiarism. Plagiarism is a complicated issue, as many students don't even realize when they are doing it. An easy way to avoid committing plagiarism is to always share another researcher's findings in your own words and cite your sources. If you have read and fully understand an article, there is no reason why you would have to lean on using the author's words instead of your own. Even when summarizing research articles in your own words, you will need to cite those sources. The easiest way to prevent plagiarism is to give credit to all of the individuals from whom you pulled your literature review information.

Writing a successful literature review is all about preparation and planning. Reading lots of good literature reviews will help you prepare. Thinking about what you want to write will also help. Finally, writing a detailed outline of your literature review is the best way to create a foundation for your own paper. You might even want to show the outline to your mentor before you write the full review. If you create an outline with all of your thoughts and research and follow it closely, it will be a lot easier to write your literature review.

When you create your full literature review (not necessarily the outline), you should also include APA subject headers to help organize your paper. Be sure to look up the different levels of APA subject headers before you create them. You should start your literature review with the introduction. The first header will look like this in your paper:

Introduction

In the introduction, I generally like to start out with what I call "the statement of the problem." The "problem" is your dependent variable, or what you will be measuring in your study. It's very important that you focus on your DV here and not your IV. For example, if your study is researching how to decrease depression with Cognitive Behavioral Therapy (CBT), your independent variable would be *CBT* and your dependent variable (a.k.a. "the problem") would be *depression*. When you create your statement of the problem, you will want to come up with an eye-catching statement that is backed up with at least two research studies that you will include as references. The purpose of this statement is to entice the reader into reading the rest of your article. It is similar to the purpose of a headline for a newspaper article. Many people will read the first sentence of your article and then decide if they want to finish reading it or move on to another article. An example of a statement of the problem for this topic might look like this:

> Depression is a pandemic in our society and leads to over $10 billion in lost work time, disability, and even death, each year (Author Last Name, 2018; Second Author Last Name, 2020).

Following this opening statement comes the rest of your introduction. The introduction is important because it provides readers with a thorough background of your DV and why it needs to be studied further. If the reader gets through the introduction and believes that it is a real problem, you have done your job. Once the introduction is complete, you can spend some time discussing other independent variables that have been used to study depression. For example, you might look at other treatments besides CBT. Your subject heading might look like this:

Treatments for Depression

Note that this level 2 header is flush left and in bold. In this section you can discuss other types of psychotherapy or even medical therapies that have effectively or ineffectively been used to treat depression. There should be lots of facts and references in this section of your paper. Once you have completed your introduction, then you move on to the more focused part of the literature review in which you examine only research related to the variables in your hypotheses. At this point, if we follow the same example, you would discuss research regarding only CBT and depression. Your next level 2 header might look like this:

Cognitive Behavioral Therapy and Depression

This section will be the bulk of your literature review and will focus only on those articles that discuss your specific hypothesis of how CBT improves depression. You will want to state the findings and share any critiques you have of each research article. Remember that every bit of information you include here must have both an in-text APA citation and a reference at the end of your paper. The majority of the articles you summarize should support your hypothesis, and those should come first. Any remaining articles that contradict your hypothesis should come after the supportive ones and near the end of the literature review.

Once you have finished reporting all of the research articles you feel are necessary for your literature review, you are ready to state your hypotheses. Be sure that your hypotheses are directional; they must indicate whether your IV *increases* or *decreases* the DV. Also, be sure that your hypotheses are always in the past tense and use third person. Here are some examples of hypothesis statements you could have for your study on CBT and depression:

> The present study hypothesized that those clients that received ten hours of Cognitive Behavioral Therapy over a ten-week period will have fewer symptoms of Major Depression compared to those that did not receive the Cognitive Behavioral Therapy.

A hypothesis can be more complex too. It might read like this.

> The present study hypothesized that men over the age of 50 would experience fewer symptoms of major depression after receiving ten weeks of Cognitive Behavioral Therapy, compared to men who did not receive any therapy. It was also hypothesized that women, regardless of age, would experience fewer symptoms of major depression after ten weeks of Cognitive Behavioral Therapy compared to women who did not receive therapy.

Your hypotheses should always be stated at the end of your introduction section, immediately before moving on to explain your study's methods.

8 Writing a Methods Section

Now that you have completed your introduction and literature review, it's time to move on to the methods section. The methods section has a very different feel from that of the introduction and literature review. The purpose of the methods section is to show your readers exactly how you conducted your study. Since you are writing in APA, remember to always write in third person, past tense. Never use words like "I," "we," "us," or "our group." Third person, past tense, uses words such as "the researchers examined" or "the team studied."

DOI: 10.4324/9781003099406-10

The methods section is all about precision and details. You must provide enough details in your writing so that another researcher can replicate or repeat your study exactly as you did it. In order to do this, you must describe the study's physical environment as well as all measurement tools that were used. Let's say that you conduct your experiment in a study room in your college library. Is it acceptable to state that the experiment was conducted in a study room in your college library? Although true, this does not provide enough detail for proper replication. What your description should say is that the experiment took place in a 4-by-6-foot study room in the college library with white walls, a table, two desk chairs, and a clock located above the door. Even though these minute details might seem useless to you, they are variables that have the potential to affect the results of a future replication of your study. On a similar note, can you just say that to measure your dependent variable of depression, you used a depression test? Again, you need more. You have to provide the name of the measurement tool you used. For instance, if you used the Beck Depression Inventory (BDI), you must reference the BDI and include reliability and validity information about the test as well as information on how often the BDI has been used in the past by other researchers. This will provide the necessary evidence to prove that the BDI is both reliable and valid.

An APA methods section has three key subsections: (1) participants, (2) apparatus, and (3) materials and procedures. When you begin writing your methods section and create each of the three subsections, be sure to use correct, APA-compliant formatting for your headings. Your first heading will look like this:

Methods

Please note that the word "Methods" is centered and in bold. That is a level 1 heading. Next, you will have a level 2 heading directly underneath the word "Methods." A level 2 heading is also bold but flush left rather than centered. Your first level 2 heading will be the word "Participants," as follows:

Participants

First and foremost, you will provide information about your study's participants. When working with humans, the term "participants" is used instead of "subjects." The term "subjects" can be used, however, if you use animals in your experiment instead of humans. You will want to include several key details, including how many people were in your study, where they were recruited from, as well as their basic demographic information. If age, race, or gender were variables included in your study, be sure to include the percentages of your participant population that fall into each group. For example, you could say that the present study included 100 participants, recruited from a medium-sized community college in Southern California. The age range was 18–36 with a mean age of 20. The sample from this study was 48% male and 52% female, 48% White, 38% Latinx, and 14% Asian American.

A participant subsection might be as short as what I have just outlined if these are the only variables of interest to your study. However, if additional pieces of information about your participants were relevant to your study, you should include them here as well. Anything that illustrates the uniqueness of your population should be documented here. When you report numbers or percentages, you always want to use the number, such as "12" rather than the word "twelve," unless the very first word of a sentence is a number. Notice the way numbers are reported in this sentence: "One hundred students participated in the study with an age range of 18–36 years old." Note that "one hundred" was spelled out, while the age range of "18–36" was given in numbers.

The next subsection is titled "Apparatus and Materials" (or just "Materials"). In this section, it's your job to thoroughly describe all the equipment, surveys, and tests used for your study. Use a level 2 header to begin this section, shown as follows:

Apparatus and Materials

Note that it is in bold and flush left on the page. Directly underneath this subheading, you will have to use a level 3 header, which further segments the "Apparatus and Materials" portion of your methods based on each of the material items. For example, let's say that you used a demographics survey to gather information about your participants. Your level 3 subject header would look like this:

Demographics Survey

Please note that demographics survey is in bold, italics, and left flush. In the paragraph titled "Demographics Survey," you should include a detailed overview of the item. For example, a demographics survey was used to collect general information about the participants. Questions on this survey included asking participants for their age, gender, ethnicity, and annual income. Please keep in mind that another researcher should be able to replicate your study using the exact same questions that you used. If there is not enough detail in your report to replicate the survey, or other measurement tools, researchers won't be able to run your study and repeat your results. Once you have completed the description of the first item, you move to the next measurement tool that you used. Be sure to start a new paragraph and use another level 3 heading, such as you see in the next section for PowerPoint slides. Once you name the item, you describe it just as you did before, with as much details as possible.

PowerPoint Slides

Participants in this study were shown a total of five PowerPoint slides. Each slide contained one of the five words, in the following order: dog, cat, bird, wolf, sheep. All slides had a blue background and the letters for each word were in white, using a Times New Roman 36-point font. Participants sat approximately one foot away from the computer when they viewed these slides.

Once you have included each and every piece of equipment (and that may include computers, food, software, study rooms, surveys, tests, sound machines, EKGs, etc.), you have finished the materials section. It's then time to move on to the final methods subsection, titled "Procedures."

Procedures

For the Procedures heading you use a level 2 heading, as seen here. I find the procedures subsection to be the most enjoyable part of the methods section to write. It's fairly straightforward. Before describing this section, I would like to start with a strong recommendation: *You will find the procedures subsection a lot easier to write if you have already run at least one participant through your entire experiment.* You can run your participant through a pilot study, a manipulation check, or the actual experiment, and once you have run at least one participant through the entire study, it will be a lot easier to write this section. If you are not familiar with pilot studies or manipulation checks, please review these topics in your textbook.

Not every student or group will have the opportunity to run a pilot study or manipulation check. However, if you or your group can run just one participant through the entire study, it will make the procedures section a lot easier to write. There are other benefits too. The first time you run your experiment, you will inevitably run into some problems. It's best to fix these problems before you recruit large groups of participants. *I would recommend grabbing one or two people from one of your classes, someone that doesn't know much about your study, and running them through the entire experiment.* That way you will be able to see what works or doesn't work, and you can also get honest feedback from your classmate on what they liked or didn't like about your study. That feedback could be invaluable, because you probably won't get it once you actually run your full experiment with strangers as your participants. Once you have run these one or two practice participants, then you can recruit the real participants for your study from the quad, other psychology classes, or whatever system your college uses.

Once you have run one or more people through your entire experiment, it is now a lot easier to write your procedures section. The purpose of this section is to write a detailed, step-by-step narration of everything that your participants do in the experiment and everything that the researchers say or do to the participants from the moment the researcher first meets the participant until the participant leaves the study. It's very important not to leave out any details, since other researchers will read and replicate your study based only on what you have written in the procedures section.

Let us give you a few other tips for writing your procedures section. The first tip is to be sure to describe how participants were assigned to conditions. For example, did you use random assignment? Second, be sure to clearly identify all of your independent, dependent, and extraneous variables. Please remember that although you are familiar with your study, your readers are not. What might seem very clear to you may not be clear to others.

Third, after you have written your procedures section, *have a psychology classmate who is not familiar with your study read your procedures section and tell you if they could replicate the entire study based on what they just read.* Chances are you will need to include more details after your classmate reads your paper. Ask them if they can envision running the entire experiment step by step. If they can do it from what you have written, you have completed the procedures.

Fourth, be sure to include any instructions that were given to participants using the exact words the researchers communicated to the participants. Remember that every participant must get the *exact* same instructions, word for word. Finally, be sure to have a step-by-step list of everything that takes place in your experiment, in the correct order, with the right amount of details so that it can be replicated. Remember our credo: There is no such thing as too many details as long as you stay focused. Once you have finished the procedures subsection, you have completed the methods section.

Part III

Conducting Your Study, Analyzing Your Data, and Finishing Your Paper

9 Conducting Your Experiment

Congratulations – you have now completed your proposal, and you been approved by the IRB. It is now *go time*! This is the moment that you have been working for. You are ready to run your research study. In some ways, this chapter will be a review, since we have already covered how to set up your experiment and create your proposal for the IRB.

Before Collecting Data

Pilot Study

Before you run your full-scale study with all of your participants, you should run a pilot study. A pilot study is a sort of practice run, like a dress rehearsal for a play or concert. First, gather a few people that you know and run them

DOI: 10.4324/9781003099406-12

through your experiment. After they have completed your study, bring them all together and start asking questions. *Did the participants know what the study was about? Did they feel comfortable throughout the process? Were they confused by any part of the study? Did it create anxiety for anyone? Were they bored?* Basically, you should conduct a focus group with the participants and see if you can find any problems with the study before you run it full-scale.

This pilot study can also be used to run a *manipulation check*. A manipulation check tests the efficacy of your experimental variable using a small sample. For example, if your independent variable was a medication, some of the participants would receive the medication while the rest got a placebo. After you run 20 people or so through your manipulation check, you can test to see if your treatment is creating the desired effect. If the pilot study brings out some problems that need to be fixed, or your manipulation check shows no efficacy of the experimental variable, then it's time to halt the experiment and fix all problems before you continue. Once you believe you have fixed those problems, you should then run another pilot test and manipulation check to see if everything runs smoothly.

Sampling

In your research methods class, you should have also learned about sampling. You should have discussed both random and nonrandom sampling, as well as the strengths and weaknesses of each. When you conduct a student research project, you are usually allowed to use a convenience sample, or another type of nonrandom sample. However, this is definitely something that you should run by your mentor. If he or she thinks that your study has publication potential, then you might want to put in the extra work to create a simple random sample.

Informed Consent and Debriefing

When running participants through your experiment, be sure to have your informed consent and debriefing procedures ready. If required by your college, you should have already put those into your IRB proposal. If not, be sure to have these ready before running your trials. Every individual will be required to sign the informed consent form before participating in the study, and each one also needs to be debriefed afterwards so they are allowed to ask questions. It is important for your participants to know that they have the right to drop out of the study at any time, and the best place to provide this information is on your informed consent form. On a rare occasion, a problem might occur with a participant during a study trial that you didn't anticipate and perhaps don't know how to handle. Be sure to contact your mentor if this happens so they can help you deal with similar situations with future trials. It is always a good idea to keep phone numbers for psychological services and campus police on hand in case you or one of your participants requires their services while running your study.

Collecting Data

Depending on the nature of your study, collecting data for a student project can take days, weeks, and sometimes months. If you are collecting data manually, be sure that every participant has a number and that all the data is organized and complete. You must be very detail-oriented and keep your data organized to be successful at research. Always have another person, perhaps your mentor, check your data to make sure it has been entered correctly. If you are conducting an online survey and you are using software like SurveyMonkey, or something similar, this process becomes much easier since the software saves the responses for you.

Post–Data Collection

Participant Incentives

It's not uncommon to provide a participant with some small incentive to be given after they have completed your study. This can help you receive a higher number of people who are interested in joining your study. If you offer your participants something, such as extra credit for a class, you must follow up with them and make sure that they receive it. As a respected researcher, you want to be portrayed as a professional by your participants, and following through with your commitments is an easy place to start.

Cleaning Up Your Data

If this is your first time running a full-scale experiment by yourself, you may never have been asked to "clean your data." Data cleaning is the process of removing errors from your data set. Cleaning involves checking and rechecking the data you entered and closely examining outliers. If you find outliers, see whether or not they are errors, and then decide how to deal with them. This is another topic to discuss with your mentor. Different researchers have different methods for dealing with this issue. Cleaning should be your final step before you start analyzing your data and writing your results section.

10 Analyzing Your Data and Writing a Results Section

At this point in your senior thesis journey, you should have run your experiment and gathered some data. Your next task will be to use your statistical knowledge to analyze, understand, and report your study's findings. This chapter begins with a discussion of the different statistical tests that you can choose

DOI: 10.4324/9781003099406-13

from to analyze your data, and when to use them. Then it will delve more into what goes into the *results* section of your senior thesis write-up as well as how to report your statistical results properly in APA format.

Before you can begin writing about your study's findings, you will need to run some statistical tests on your raw data. Hopefully you are already familiar with the different types of statistical tests, as they will be covered only briefly here. If not, it may be a good idea to sit down with your mentor and discuss some of the areas in which you feel you are lacking. This chapter contains information on *chi-square, correlation, t-test, regression,* and *ANOVA* (including *one-way, factorial, repeated measures,* and *mixed* designs), which may be helpful for you in deciding which test(s) you need to use to analyze your data.

Chi-Square

There are two types of chi-square tests that can be used. The first is a *goodness of fit* test, in which your observed data values are compared to their expected values in order to determine if your data is representative of the target population. The second chi-square test you can use is a *test of independence.* This type of chi-square will determine any differences among groups in your data (e.g., sex – male vs. female). It can be used only when each of your data's categories are completely independent of one another, meaning that there is no crossover between your groups. Due to the nature of these tests, you will most likely use the chi-square test of independence much more often than the goodness of fit test when having to do it by hand. The good thing about using statistical software such as SPSS to run the *Pearson chi-square* is that it automatically runs both tests for you. The following is a list of values you will need to be knowledgeable of and able to interpret when running a chi-square test.

> *Chi-square (X^2) statistic*: The value that will result from your chi-square test. This value is compared to the values in a chi-square critical value table to determine, based on your degrees of freedom, if it is significant.
> *Degrees of Freedom (df)*: A number that represents how much variance is allowed – based on the number of values – in a statistical analysis.
> *Sample Size (N)*: The number of participants included in a statistical analysis.
> *P-Value (p)*: A value that is compared to a set significance level (usually $p = .05$) to determine if the results of a statistical test are significant. If $p < .05$, then it is considered significant. However, if $p > .05$, then it is not significant.

Test of Independence:

Hypotheses

- H_0: (*variable A*) and (*variable B*) are independent.
- H_A: (*variable A*) and (*variable B*) are not independent.

Degrees of Freedom

- $df = (k - 1)$
- "*k*" is the number of *categories*

Results Statement

- The relationship between (*variable A*) and (*variable B*) is/is not statistically significant, $X^2(df, N) = $ *chi-square value*, $p = $ *p-value*.

Example: You are performing a study on teenagers (ages 13 to 17) to determine if daily caloric intake significantly differs between males and females.

Hypotheses

- H_0: *Biological sex* and *daily caloric intake* are independent.
- H_A: *Biological sex* and *daily caloric intake* are not independent.

X^2 Statistic

- $X^2 = 5.32$

Degrees of Freedom

- $do = (k - 1)$
  $df = (2 - 1)$
  $df = 1$

P-Value

- $p = .027$

Results Statement

- The relationship between *gender* and *daily caloric intake* in teenagers is statistically significant, $X^2(1, 50) = 5.32$, $p = .03$.

Correlation

A *correlation* is a statistical test that is used to identify directional associations among variables. Although I am almost positive you have been told this at least once or twice before reading it here, *correlation does not imply causation*. A correlational relationship can claim only that there is a positive, negative, or nonexisting association between two or more variables. It cannot, however, back up the claim that one variable has *caused* another to change or trend in a particular way. Similar to the chi-square test of independence, you will need to have a few pieces of information, this time including a new statistic: "*r*."

> *Correlation Coefficient (r)*: A coefficient of either positive or negative value given from a statistical test for correlation that indicates the strength and direction of an association between variables. A correlation's strength is given by how close the *r* value is to 0 or $+/-$ 1. An *r* value closer to $+/-$ 1 is considered stronger than one closer to 0. A positive *r* value indicates that when one variable increases, so does the other. A negative *r* value indicates an inverse relationship in which one variable increases while the other decreases.
>
> *Effect Size*: A classification of the strength of a correlation based on a scale derived from the value of the correlation coefficient. Various scales exist based on different statistical research findings, and depending on which one you use, the cutoff values may change. But as I used in my advanced statistical course, and according to the work of Cohen (1988, 1992), here are some accurate values that can be used to determine effect size:

- $r = 0.1$ (small)
- $r = 0.3$ (medium)
- $r = 0.5$ (strong)

Hypotheses

- H_0: The correlation coefficient of (*variable A*) and (*variable B*) is equal to zero.
- H_A: The correlation coefficient of (*variable A*) and (*variable B*) is not equal to zero.

Degrees of Freedom

- $df = N - 2$

Results Statement

- There was a (*effect size*) (*direction*) correlation between (*variable A*) and (*variable B*), $r(df) = r$ statistic, $p = p\text{-}value$.

Example: You and some fellow researchers are conducting a study on the relationship between ice cream sales and drowning instances in the summertime.

Hypotheses

- H_0: The correlation coefficient of *ice cream sales* and *drowning instances* is equal to zero.

- H_A: The correlation coefficient of *ice cream sales* and *drowning instances* is not equal to zero.

Correlation Coefficient

- $r = .89$

Degrees of Freedom

- $df = N - 2$
  $df = 100 - 2$
  $df = 98$

P-Value

- $p = .00001$

Results Statement

- There was a strong positive correlation between *ice cream sales* and *drowning instances*, $r(98) = .89$, $p < .001$.

T-Test

The purpose of a *t*-test is to determine the differences between mean values within a data set. Depending on what your data looks like, you will have to perform one of three different types: (1) one-sample, (2) independent sample, or (3) paired sample. The one-sample *t*-test is used when you are interested in comparing the mean of one sample within your data to one absolute value (usually an already-established mean value found outside of your data). The independent samples *t*-test would be used instead if you wanted to compare the means of two completely independent groups within your data. And a paired sample *t*-test is used to compare the means of one group within your data at two different time points. An example of an independent samples *t*-test follows.

Independent Samples T-Test

Hypotheses

- H_0: The means of (*group A*) and (*group B*) are equal.
- H_A: The means of (*group A*) and (*group B*) are not equal.

Degrees of Freedom

- $df = N - 2$

Results Statement

- There was/was not a statistically significant difference in the mean (*dependent variable*) between (*group 1*) and (*group 2*), $t(df) = $ *t-value*, $p = $ *p-value*.

Example: You are running a study to determine if the mean IQ value for high school students differs between lowerclassmen (9th and 10th grades) and upperclassmen (11th and 12th grades).

Hypotheses

- H_0: The mean IQ values of *lowerclassmen* and *upperclassmen* are equal.
- H_A: The mean IQ values of *lowerclassmen* and *upperclassmen* are not equal.

T-*Value*

- $t = 1.285$

Degrees of Freedom

- $df = N - 2$
  $df = 2000 - 2$
  $df = 1998$

P-*Value*

- $p = .337$

Results Statement

- There was not a statistically significant difference in the mean *IQ* between high school *lowerclassmen* and *upperclassmen*, $t(1998) = 1.29$, $p = .33$.

ANOVA

Analysis of variance (ANOVA) tests are similar to the *t*-test in that they indicate statistically significant differences between mean values. Where ANOVA differs is in its ability to compare means for more than two variables at one time. Its results will indicate if there is overall significance between your variables, including what are called *interaction effects* occurring between the tested groups. What an ANOVA test alone fails to tell you is exactly where the significance is coming from among your tested variables. To find that out, you would have to run a post-hoc test to follow up your original findings, which I will cover later in this chapter.

Many types of ANOVA tests exist. However, the main ones you may want to consider using for your research project are one-way, two-way, repeated measures, and analysis of covariance (ANCOVA). A *one-way ANOVA* is run on data that has only two variables, one dependent and one independent. In a one-way analysis, the independent variable must have two or more independent groups which can be compared to one another. For example, a study interested in understanding the effects of different forms of exercise on feelings of self-worth could run a one-way ANOVA on self-worth and different types of exercise such as walking, swimming, and weightlifting. In this example, *feelings of self-worth* acts as the dependent variable while *exercise* is the independent variable. Exercise was broken up into three subcategories or groups, and these become the levels within the one-way analysis whose mean values are compared to one another.

A *two-way ANOVA* is similar in that it still compares mean values between variables, but it includes two independent variables instead of one. This analysis additionally evaluates what is known as an *interaction*, which indicates whether the effects of the first independent variable influence the effects of the second independent variable on the dependent variable, and vice versa. For example, let's say you are running a study to see if sugar intake and/or amount of nightly sleep have any effects on concentration levels in college students while in a classroom setting. Your sugar intake variable consists of two groups (high sugar and low sugar), while your sleep variable consists of three groups (< 6 hours, 6–8 hours, > 8 hours). A two-way ANOVA would indicate main effects (whether either of the two variables have an effect on student concentration in the classroom) as well as any possible interaction effects (e.g., do the effects of sugar intake influence how nightly sleep effects concentration?). A one- or two-way ANOVA can become a *repeated measures ANOVA (rmANOVA)* when only one group of participants is used for all of the variable conditions, just at different points in time. An rmANOVA can only be used if the effects of the earlier conditions do not carry over and effect the later conditions.

Now, let's say that after running your experiment, you identified one or more variables other than your independent variable(s) that you think may have had an influence on your dependent variable. In this case you may want to run an *analysis of covariance*, also called an *ANCOVA*. An ANCOVA measures differences in mean values after adjusting for these confounding variables, which are also called *covariates*. This is an important statistical method to utilize when there is a possibility of covariates hiding within your data, as they have the potential to alter your results and bring you to draw the wrong conclusions.

These ANOVA tests are vast in their abilities; however, they do have limits. For example, they can only tell you if there is a significant overall effect between your variables. They cannot indicate on their own which variables are responsible for the (in)significant findings. The same holds true for interactions; if there was an interaction found between your two independent variables, the two-way ANOVA would not be able to indicate the mechanisms behind that interaction. In other words, if we went back to the sugar and sleep example, you would know that there was an interaction occurring between sugar intake, amount of sleep, and concentration levels, but you would not have any indication as to which of those variables were driving the interaction. In order to evaluate this, a follow-up *post-hoc* test and/or some *simple effects testing* would have to be used.

Many types of post-hoc tests are used in statistics today, including: Fisher's LSD, Tukey HSD, Scheffe, and Bonferroni. *Fisher's LSD* is the most lenient of these tests, and therefore is often avoided unless an adjusted alpha level is calculated and used (again, something you will probably not run into until advanced statistics). The *Bonferroni* test is often used instead; however, many professors from higher-level statistics courses have recently criticized it as being too conservative. *Scheffe's* test is also known to be strict, but it can be very useful when you have groups of unequal sizes. Lastly, the *Tukey HSD* test tends to fall in the middle with regard to stringency and is often used along with the Bonferroni test. All of these can be utilized in whichever statistics program you use, so if you find an interaction effect in your initial data analysis, be sure to take this one step further and use a post-hoc test to determine which variable(s) are driving your interaction.

Another way to analyze an interaction effect is by using *simple effects testing*. Just like the post-hoc tests we previously discussed, simple effects testing helps you determine what is driving an interaction to occur; however, it does so by repartitioning variance. In other words, you would isolate each group in your data and compare each mean value to see which one(s) are causing the interaction to occur. Due to a heightened risk of error in this type of testing, it is best to always use the Scheffe test since it is the strictest and will therefore do the best job of eliminating error. The simple effects Scheffe test is done by hand, using data values generated into your original ANOVA summary table (after running the basic ANOVA analysis). You can always ask your mentor for more information on this type of statistical testing if you think that your experiment's results could benefit from it.

Hypotheses – Main Effects

- H_0: There are no differences in (*DV*) based on (*IV*).
- H_A: There are differences in (*DV*) based on (*IV*).

★*Note*: If you are running a factorial ANOVA, you will have several sets of hypothesis statements: one for each independent variable that is included in the analysis as well as any existing covariates.

Hypotheses – Interaction

- H_0: There are no differences in (*DV*) based on the interaction of (IV_1) and (IV_2).
- H_A: There are differences in (*DV*) based on the interaction of (IV_1) and (IV_2).

Degrees of Freedom

- $df = N - k$
- k is the number of samples

Results Statements

- Main Effects:
  There was/was not a statistically significant effect of (IV) on (DV), $F(df_1, df_2)$ = F-value, p = ____, η^2 = ____.
- Interaction:
  There was/was not a statistically significant interaction between (IV_1) and (IV_2) on (DV).

Multiple Regression

Multiple regression is used when you are interested in forming predictions based on a particular set of variables. The first thing to note about this type of test is that it is based on correlation, so you must first run a correlational analysis in order for this one to be utilized. When running a regression analysis, your independent variable(s) are considered the "predictors" and your dependent variable is the "criterion," all of which must be continuous variables (with the exception of the predictor variables, which can be dichotomous). There are three approaches to regression that you can use: (1) standard, (2) hierarchical, and (3) statistical. The *standard* approach is a "forced-entry" approach, meaning that all your predictor variables are entered into the analysis at the same time in order to determine the extent to which each variable contributes to the overall relationship. The *hierarchical* approach allows for more control, as you can layer each of your predictor variables into the analysis in a hierarchical order of your choosing – similar to how you would enter covariates into an ANCOVA.

The last form of regression you can use is the *statistical* approach, which is a computer-controlled method of running a regression in which you can choose from three different options: (a) the backward approach, (b) the forward approach, or (c) the stepwise approach. In the *backward* approach, all your variables are thrown into the regression analysis at the same time but then removed one by one based on their significance level (lowest significance level removed first). This limits the number of predictors that are included in your overall analysis. When you choose the *forward* approach, each of your variables will be entered one at a time starting with your variable with the highest Pearson correlation. The *stepwise* approach is by far the most exploratory, as it combines both the backward and forward approaches. It begins by using the forward approach for the first two variables, and then it switches to the backward approach in order to throw out any nonsignificant variables from your analysis. All three forms of the statistical approach can be useful to you if you choose to run a multiple regression analysis based on the statistical approach.

Figures – Tables and Graphs

After analyzing your data from the statistical testing, you may then want to make some visual aids to help your readers better understand the results. The types of visual aids most commonly used in research articles are tables and graphs. When creating tables and graphs, it is important to follow the formatting guidelines from APA (or BPS, if that is what your professor prefers), as it will outline how the figure should look. What is included in your table or graph will be entirely contingent upon the nature of your study; however, a lot of studies will include data values that display the statistical significance of each variable including means, standard deviations, and *p*-values. Other values that are often included in tables in particular are the *N* (sample size) and the statistical coefficient, whether it is a *t*, *r*, or *F* value.

Table 10.1 is an example of a table portraying data from a hypothetical study, evaluating any associations between the overall instances of adultery confessed by married couples and other variables such as age, self-esteem, locus of control, and relationship satisfaction. The data provided in Table 10.1 are hypothetical only and do not represent results from an actual study.

Now here is an example of an entire results section as well as some graphs that Lindsay produced back in her undergraduate studies as a student in a biopsychology class. While in that class, she and her fellow students participated in a study ran by her professor, after which they were asked to analyze it and provide results. In the study, each student's blood glucose levels were measured at four different time points after ingesting a food item containing either high-fructose corn syrup or natural sugar. The figures in Table 10.1 were made to display any relationships found between time, the type of food eaten, and the participants' biological sex.

Table 10.1 Correlations Between Instances of Adultery and Age, Self-Esteem, Relationship Satisfaction, and Locus of Control Measures

Variable		SD	N	R	Sig. 2-tailed
Age	22.48	7.46	196	−.149	.034★
Self-Esteem	3.27	.41	198	−.202	.003★
LOC Internality	4.86	.64	198	−.178	.018★
LOC Powerful Others	2.99	.77	198	.191	.010★
LOC Chance	2.85	.68	198	.222	.002★
Relationship Satisfaction	7.71	1.34	198	.100	.126
Instances of Adultery	3.55	1.05	198		

★*p* < .05

Results

A mixed-design ANOVA was conducted using the IBM SPSS Statistics software to determine whether there were statistically significant differences in blood glucose levels based on the main and interaction effects of gender, food condition, and time. All assumptions were presumed met based on preliminary data analysis. The results indicated blood glucose levels to be the highest on average at T1 (148.18 ± 16.27), which occurred 20 minutes following food consumption (see Figure 10.1 for overall average blood glucose levels). The main effect of time resulted in a statistically significant difference in blood glucose levels,

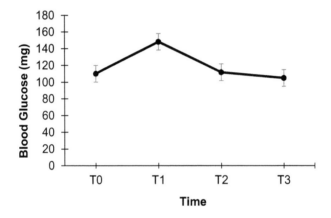

Figure 10.1 Overall mean blood glucose levels over the four time measurement points. Significant differences were found between the effects of time on blood glucose levels. Standard error of the means are represented in the figure by the error bars attached to each time point.

$F(3) = 9.56$, $p < .001$, with T1 showing significant mean differences between T0 ($p < .001$), T2 ($p = .008$), and T3 ($p < .001$). Individuals assigned to the No HFCS food condition had the highest average blood glucose levels (153.20 ± 17.08) compared to the HFCS group (144 ± 15.80) indicated at T1 (see Figure 10.2 for average blood glucose levels based on food condition). The main effect for food condition resulted in a statistically nonsignificant difference in blood glucose levels, $F(1, 8) = .52$, $p = .49$. Average blood glucose levels were recorded highest for females at T1 (149.40 ± 16.61), as indicated in Figure 10.3. The main effect of gender resulted in a statistically nonsignificant difference in blood glucose levels, $F(1, 8) = 2.55$, $p = .14$. The interaction effect between food condition and time resulted in a nonsignificant difference in blood glucose levels, $F(3,) = 1.96$, $p = .14$.

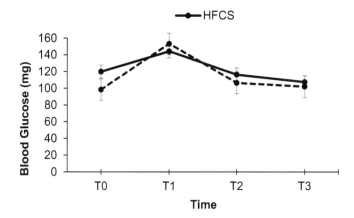

Figure 10.2 Mean blood glucose levels for the HFCS group and the No HFCS group, at all four measurement time points. No blood glucose level differences were found based on the effects of food condition group membership. Standard errors are represented in the figure by the error bars attached to each time point.

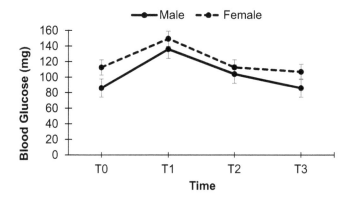

Figure 10.3 Mean blood glucose levels for both males and females at each measurement time point. No differences in blood glucose levels were found based on the effects of gender. Standard error of the means are represented in the figure by the error bars attached to each time point.

References

Cohen, J. (1988). *Statistical Power Analysis for the Behavioral Sciences* (2nd ed.). Hillside, NJ: Lawrence Erlbaum Associates.

Cohen, J. (1992). A power primer. *Psychological Bulletin*, 112, 155–159. doi: 10.1037/0033-2909.112.1.155

11 Writing a Discussion Section

The *discussion* section immediately follows your study's results. The discussion section still has several rules to follow, but far less than any other section in the paper. In my opinion, the discussion section is the more enjoyable section to write because you get to talk about your results in more casual, easy-to-understand language. You make your case as to why your results are important for the world to know about. It allows for a bit more creativity than the other sections you have already written, since you can be more flexible with the content.

What should be found in a discussion? The first thing that should be included here is a restatement of your study's main findings. You can start the discussion by restating your hypotheses and then noting whether those hypotheses were supported by your study's findings. You will want to use plain language to demonstrate your results in a more well-understood manner than what was provided in your results. In the discussion section, you should focus on words and descriptions rather than on numbers and values.

One way to think about your discussion section is as the opposite of your literature review. In the literature review, you start out with a general topic and end up with a very narrow and focused hypothesis by the end of it. In the discussion section, you start off with the narrow hypothesis, and whether it was supported, and then you more broadly explain the findings of your study. Here is an example for how to start your discussion section:

DOI: 10.4324/9781003099406-14

The present study examined the influence of exercise on the energy level of teenage boys. It was hypothesized that a 30-minute exercise regimen would enhance the energy level of all the boys. Results demonstrated that boys between 13 and 16 who completed the 30-minute workout described in this study had significantly more energy than the boys who did not complete the workout. However, the boys between the ages of 16 and 18 who completed the 30-minute workout showed no improvement in energy level compared to those that did not complete the workout. Thus, the hypothesis was only partially confirmed as only the younger group of boys showed evidence of benefiting from the exercise regimen.

The next point you should discuss is how the results of your study relate to the research you discussed in the literature review. If your current results replicated the results of some of the previous studies cited, discuss the similarities between those studies and your results. If your results were different from previous studies, explain why you think that your results did not match up with the studies you listed in the literature review. Be sure to reference the previous literature from the literature review when you mention it again in the discussion section. For example:

The results of the present study were similar to the study conducted by Jones (2018) discussed earlier. Both studies noted that younger teenage boys benefitted more from the short exercise workout compared to older teenage boys. This finding might have occurred because the boys selected for the current study used the exact same workout as the boys in the Jones (2018) study.

If your study found something different from research discussed in your literature review, be sure to explain any reasons why this could have occurred:

The current study demonstrated different results from the work of Smith et al. (2019). The current study displayed a significant benefit for younger teenage boys who completed an exercise workout, whereas the Smith et al. (2019) study did not show that same benefit. One possible explanation for this difference is a difference in each study's population used. The current study included high school students from a large, urban high school while the Smith et al. (2019) study included students from a small rural high school. It's possible that differences in diet, culture, or physical activity outside of school significantly altered the present study's results.

Once you have thoroughly stated your findings and how they were similar to and/or different from the previous literature, you might want to note any unique findings of your study that have not already been noted in the discussion section. For example, perhaps the exercise regimen you implemented caused some negative impact on your teens. Maybe those who didn't participate in the exercise intervention had negative results other than reduction in energy. It's entirely possible that you didn't have any unique findings or that those findings were already covered when you discuss how your results were different from those of previous research cited.

After stating the differences or uniqueness of your study, you will then have a chance to focus on what your results actually mean for the rest of the world. How do your results generalize and help people outside of your study? If the purpose of research is to improve our understanding of people and help provide avenues for living fuller lives, then this is your opportunity to show that your study does just that. For instance, your study found that younger teenage boys benefitted from the short workout, while older teenage boys did not. How can we use these results practically to benefit schoolchildren?

> It was stated earlier that younger teenage boys benefitted from the exercise workout and older teenage boys did not. This new information could be used to reshape the way that physical education is taught and practiced in grade school environments. For example, the present study showed that in large city-based urban high schools, 30-minute exercise workouts were more beneficial for younger teenage boys than older teenage boys. This indicated that perhaps the school's exercise program should only be implemented for the population that it has been shown to benefit and new research should be conducted to find what is beneficial for the older teenage boys. Keeping that in mind, though, Smith's (2018) research showed that a 30-minute regimen was beneficial to all high school–age boys if they were in a rural setting. So, the key takeaway from this current study is that location matters. Boys growing up in more urban areas have different needs from those of young boys growing up in a more rural setting.

The next part of your discussion will include the limitations of your research study. Here you will want to include what went wrong with your study or what should have been done differently. It could have been something you would have liked to do but was simply not possible due to your budget, available sample, or other issues. For example, let's say that the sample you selected for your study was not a true random sample, was small, and might have included only a very specific demographic compared to the rest of your state or country. You would want to identify all of these flaws at this point in your write-up. Topics that can be included while talking about your study's limitations include: the sample size, recruitment strategies, the demographic of your sample, time restrictions, budgetary restrictions, equipment failures, tests or measures lacking sensitivity, flawed surveys, flaws in your design, and problems while running your experiment. Here is an example of how you should report your study's limitations:

> Apart from the unique findings of this research, there were also some limitations. This research was conducted at a medium-sized high school in California in a primarily residential neighborhood. The demographics were

slightly skewed in this region in comparison to other, more urban-based high schools in California. This high school had a larger representation of Anglo and Latinx students than African American and Asian American. Also, the sample taken was a convenience sample which was limited to only 40 teenage boys. Another limitation of this study was the test used to measure the teens' "energy level." Although the test was well standardized, it was more heavily standardized on adults rather than teens or children. This lack of standardization on teens could lead to inaccuracies. Finally, due to time limitations, this study was performed as a cross-sectional study rather than a longitudinal study. So, the current researchers were only able to track the teens' behavior over a two-week period rather than the previously mentioned research, which monitored the teens over a three-month period of time.

The final topic covered in most discussion sections has to do with future research that will be conducted by the current researchers. Some call this the "Where do we go from here?" portion of the discussion. This section takes the findings of the current research and uses them to build the next study that this same group of researchers will conduct. It might look like this:

Based on the unique findings of this study, the present researchers plan to engage in several future studies. The first study will focus on the differences in the efficacy of exercise programs between urban and rural teenage boys. The second study will examine the differences in the effectiveness of exercise in younger vs. older teen age boys. The current research team may also examine the effectiveness of exercise in younger and older teenage girls in both rural and urban populations.

12 Final Touches
Title Page, Abstract, and Checklists

Congratulations! You have almost completed your senior thesis project. At this point you have written your literature review, methods, results, and discussion. This chapter will focus on putting the finishing touches on your paper, including creating a title page and an abstract. After discussing these two topics, we will look at some checklists you can use to make sure that your paper has all the required elements.

Creating a Professional Title Page

If you conduct an Internet search on how to create an APA title page, you might find instructions on how to complete both a student and a professional title page. The two types of pages are similar, but the professional page is preferable. The first thing you will need to do when creating a professional title page is to insert a shortened version of your paper's title as a running head. The running head, along with page numbers, will appear on the title page first but will be present on every following page of your document as well.

DOI: 10.4324/9781003099406-15

Once you have created your running head and page numbers, the rest is easy. The next step is to add in the full title of your paper, the names of all the authors (first, middle initial, and last), and any affiliations (college where you attend/work). The title of your paper is placed about three to four rows down from the top of the page, centered, and boldface, and you should capitalize the major words of the title. For the author names, leave one double space blank line between the title and the author's name, center author's names on its own line. If there are two authors, use the word "and" between the names. If there are three or more authors, put a comma after each name and the word "and" before the last name.

For the authors' affiliations, skip to the next line and list the name of your department, followed by a comma, and then the name of your college or university. The final part of the title page is known as the *authors note*. For a senior thesis project you will most likely not be required to include this, but be sure to check with your mentor. Here is an example of what a professional APA title page might look like:

The Effects of Cognitive Behavioral Therapy on Major Depression:

A Clinical Study

Ross A. Seligman
Department of Psychology, Citrus College
Lindsay A. Mitchell
Department of Psychology, California State University, Fullerton

---

Figure 12.2

Now that you have completed your APA title page, your next task is to create an abstract for your paper. An abstract is, in short, a 250-word summary of your paper. You should have about one to two sentences for each section of your paper (introduction, methods, results, and discussion). The abstract is much simpler to write after all of the other sections have already been written, so be sure to do this last. The abstract should always get its own page and be found immediately following your title page. It cannot be any longer than 250 words, so be concise in your wording. Below your abstract are some keywords for the reader to note. You will want to include three to five key words that would help a reader find your article in a database.

In the abstract, you don't need any in-text references or descriptions of statistical tests. The goal is to provide readers with a brief, nontechnical overview of your paper that properly conveys its aims and findings. Here is an example of what an abstract might look like:

Abstract

Depression is a problem that affects millions of Americans on a daily basis and depletes the economy of billions of dollars due to missed work, medical expenses, and reduced productivity. One of the best nonmedical treatments for depression is Cognitive Behavioral Therapy (CBT). CBT has previously shown to be effective in two major studies. The present study used the experimental method and examined 300 male and female adult clients diagnosed with Major Depressive Disorder. Half of all the patients received CBT, whereas the other half received no therapy at all. Results of this experiment demonstrated a significant drop in depression among those in the CBT group. Results from this study can be used to help adult male and female depression patients improve their quality of life without the need for drug therapy.

Keywords: Depression, cognitive behavioral therapy, treatment

Figure 12.3

Now that you have created your title page and abstract, your paper should be complete. The final step is to go through the checklist that follows to make sure you have all of the formatting and information that are required for this paper. Once you have completed the checklist, your paper is ready to be submitted to your mentor.

General formatting issues for the entire paper
- 1" margins on all four sides.
- APA allows various accessible fonts. I typically use: Times New Roman 12+ point font
- Double space all lines.
- Text should be left justified unless otherwise indicated (such as for title page and headings).
- Indent the start of all paragraphs, with few exceptions (such as the abstract).
- Write in past tense, third person. Please do not use words such as I, we, us, our group, etc.

Title Page
- Title page has running head (with appropriate capitalization) and page number.

- Title of paper reflects what the study is about.
- Title includes the independent and dependent variables.
- Your name(s) and affiliation(s) are on the title page.
- Title of paper is centered on the page and in bold.
- Authors' names are centered on the page, underneath the title.
- Authors' affiliations are centered underneath the authors names.
- Authors note is usually optional for a research methods class.

Abstract

- Abstract states the problem that needs to be investigated by the researcher.
- Hypothesis is included.
- A brief statement about results is present.
- You have included an explanation of why the results are relevant and how they can be used.
- The abstract is between 150 and 250 words and contains at least three key words.
- The abstract is on page two with a page number and running head at the top of the page.

Introduction

- Starts on a new page – Page #3.
- Includes the title of the paper as a level 1 heading.
- Did not use the title "Introduction" for this section.
- The statement of the problem (the dependent variable) is present near the beginning of the paper.
- You have included a logical reason for why this topic is important and should be studied.
- Recent scholarly research from the last five years is used.
- Every fact taken from the research is correctly referenced in APA style.
- No Internet research is used unless allowed by your professor.
- Hypothesis or hypotheses are clearly stated in past tense, third person.
- Hypotheses state the relationship and direction of the effect between the independent and dependent variables.

Method

- Participants are thoroughly described in the participants subsection.
- Include the number of participants (using correct format for numbers), where and how they were recruited, and all relevant demographics gathered for the participants.
- In the materials subsection, you have named and described all tests, measures, surveys, equipment, software, computers, etc. You have a

paragraph for each item and a bold face header to name the tests, measure, and equipment. You included reliability and validity information where needed.

- If you have items in the appendix of your paper, you have noted where to find them.
- In the design subsection, you have identified the independent and dependent variables. You also describe how the experiment was designed to test the hypothesis and control any possible confounding variables. You have described the statistical tests that you are using.
- If you had missing or uneven data, explain why.
- Your procedures subsection is so detailed that another researcher could repeat your study *exactly as you did it*, right down to the room, tests, videos, and surveys. Every step that you did was included in order of occurrence. Please break up longer procedures sections into multiple paragraphs.

Results

- You started with a restatement of each hypothesis and indicated whether they were supported or not. Your hypotheses have direction which means that they state if the independent variable increased or decreased the dependent variable.
- All the relevant descriptive statistics are included, such as means, frequencies, N, n, and standard deviations.
- All inferential statistics are reported in APA format.
- It is noted if between or within-subjects design was used (if relevant).
- You have noted if graphs, or charts are in the appendix.
- P-values are in APA format, even if not significant.
- You have not used phrases such as "the hypothesis was proven." Be careful about strong or incorrect language. Instead use words like "The results demonstrated."

Discussion

- You have restated the basic research questions and conclusions.
- Results are explained in terms of their relevance to society. What do they mean? How can they be used to help people in the "real world"?
- You have stated what went wrong in the study. What were the limitations? Discuss flaws in the study that you couldn't avoid (or maybe you could), such as sample size, equipment failure, biases in the sample, etc.
- Based on the findings of this study, you have stated what the topic or hypothesis of your next study will look like.

References

- You have started on a new page for the Reference section.
- The word "References" is listed at the top of the page, capitalized and in bold.
- All references are in APA format. You have looked up how to reference journal articles with one or more authors. You have looked up formatting changes for open access journals, books, or other sources.
- You correctly indented the first line of each reference.
- You have alphabetized your list of references by the *first author's last name*.
- If you had two or more works by the same author, they should be ordered by publication date, with the oldest entry listed first.
- Everything is double spaced and follows APA format.
- You did not include references in this section that were not used in the paper.

Appendices – for graphs, figures, surveys, etc.

- All figures are formatted and captioned according to APA, 7th edition.
- All items in the appendix are also noted in the paper (for example – "see graph 1 in appendix 1").
- You have proofread your entire paper for spelling, grammar, and APA formatting.

13 Presenting Your Findings

One thing that I have learned in my years of teaching is that students fear public speaking more than any other type of assignment. I think that Jerry Seinfeld summed up this fear best when he said:

> According to most studies, people's number one fear is public speaking. Number two is death. Death is number two. Does that sound right? This means to the average person, if you go to a funeral, you're better off in the casket than doing the eulogy.
>
> (Goodreads Inc., 2020)

Public speaking is stressful for just about everyone, even teachers, and the only way to overcome that stress and improve your public speaking skills is to practice. As much as you might dread it, try to take advantage of any opportunities

DOI: 10.4324/9781003099406-16

that your professors might offer you to give a speech, especially if it's in a safe setting like a small group or classroom in front of your friends and peers. The reality is that giving an oral presentation is something that you will be doing throughout your life. Most jobs will require it, and college is the best place to learn and practice this skill.

There are typically two parts to presenting your paper. First, you will need to verbally deliver your information, and second, you will want to have some sort of visual display such as a poster or PowerPoint presentation. This chapter will give you some practical tips for both delivering a successful speech as well as creating a good PowerPoint presentation or poster.

The honest truth is that an audience, no matter who is in it, does not usually enjoy hearing an individual spew a bunch of facts at them. Even if the facts themselves are interesting, an audience wants to be entertained. If you can put the audience in a good mood, they are more likely to enjoy your presentation and more likely to remember what you have said. Like so many other forms of communication, what you say is just as important as how you say it. You could be sharing something as boring as the location of the local library, but if you do it in a fun way, your audience may actually remember you as well as what you said. Audiences also tend to have very short attention spans. Overwhelming them with facts and figures will most likely exhaust them and lead them to lose interest. So, when you give a speech with lots of information, it's important to balance out that information with stories and examples that capture an audience's attention and entertain them.

Hearing that you should learn to be an entertainer might not be what you wanted to hear about successful public speaking, but it is a helpful skill that will give you a leg up on your peers. If you learn to have fun with your presentations, you may find that you also feel more successful and learn to fear it less each time you do it. If you can bring out people's emotions, the information given in your speech will have a higher chance of being remembered. For these reasons, the rest of this chapter focuses on how to be more entertaining when you speak publicly.

One very easy thing to try when presenting your study to others is to speak loudly. When I feel nervous, I am able to combat it by speaking more loudly, as it allows me to burn off some of that energy. It also adds some life to the presentation, rather than boring people to sleep with a low or monotone voice. Speaking in a higher volume also makes your voice sound less shaky (which is always nice) and helps get your audience's attention.

Telling stories is also very important in a speech. It makes your speech more interesting and allows your audience to connect more effortlessly with you. Audiences don't want to listen to 20 minutes about *t*-tests and correlations. They would rather hear about some personal experiences you had while you ran your experiment, especially if you have some humorous ones that can be told in a sensitive and respectful way. I remember one group in my own research methods class years ago who did a study on the topic of beauty and self-esteem. During their presentation they told this story about how during the experiment, they showed pictures of attractive women to several female participants. One female participant, upon seeing these pictures, put down the sandwich she was eating for lunch and stated that she needed to go on a diet. Although that might be painful to hear, those are the types of stories that make your presentation real. What about telling jokes? You might have heard that you should start a presentation by telling a joke. For this type of presentation, I would actually strongly disagree with this approach. Jokes might sound like a good starting point, but they run the risk of coming off as insensitive due to the nature of the research we are doing.

By far the most important tip that I can give you about delivering an effective presentation is to practice the speech as much as you can before you deliver it to your target audience. I would recommend that you practice your entire speech in a private setting at least a couple of times. If you rehearse your presentation enough, you will be able to commit it to memory, and when you get nervous during the presentation, you hopefully won't trip on your words as much. After you rehearse it at home, you should practice it in a classroom or a setting similar to where you will be delivering the real presentation. One problem with practicing an oral presentation in your home is that you will be more relaxed and you will speak more slowly, so the presentation will last longer than when you are in front of the class. When you get in front of the class and your adrenaline starts to flow, you may speak more quickly and rush through it. After practicing at home and in a classroom, the final step is to practice in front of a small group of family members or friends. That will raise the pressure just a little bit. If everything goes as expected with a small group of friends and/or family as your audience, then you should be in good shape when it comes time to share your findings in front of a real audience.

When giving presentations of your study's findings, maintain as much eye contact with your audience as you can. This can be challenging because maintaining eye contact makes a lot of public speakers more nervous. But, if you don't scan the audience and connect with them, they may begin to feel disconnected with what you are saying and lose interest. Truth be told, it is not that fun to watch a speaker who just looks at their notes the entire time. One trick you might find useful if you find it too difficult to make eye contact with various audience members is to look at their foreheads instead. From even a close distance it will seem like you are looking them in the eye, and you will be able to better focus on what you are saying instead of how uncomfortable it makes you to make eye contact with them.

Visual Presentations

Now that we have discussed some tips for speaking in front of the class, it is now time to talk about visual displays, such as PowerPoints and posters. As a professor, I always require a PowerPoint presentation that corresponds with my students' speeches. While many professors require a PowerPoint presentation, others prefer a poster presentation. I will start by giving tips for how to give a good PowerPoint presentation, for which some clear rules should be followed. After that, we will discuss posters.

PowerPoint Presentations

There are a few common rules to follow when making PowerPoints. The first rule is to put as little information on your PowerPoint slides as you can while also clearly portraying the information you need. Putting too much information into your slides is often referred to as "death by PowerPoint." When death by PowerPoint occurs, your audience is unable to pay attention to what you are saying due to their feeling that they have to spend all their time reading what is on your slides. Include only the skeleton of the information you will be discussing and provide the rest verbally. The important thing to remember is that a PowerPoint presentation is a brief outline for your speech that should be used only as a minor guide to keep your ideas on track. Each slide should have only a few words on it; as a general rule, no more than four bullet points should be included on a single PowerPoint slide, and each bullet point should have no more than four words. In short, less is more. You can say as much as you want in your presentation, but you don't need to write your entire speech on a slide. Otherwise, people won't be listening to what you are saying, and all of the effort you may have been putting into being entertaining will fly right out the window.

Font size is very important in a PowerPoint presentation as well. Use a very large, clear font type, such as a 36 pt. Times New Roman. My advice is to use only font sizes of 24 pt. or larger, as anything smaller become difficult to read (especially for audience members in the back of the room). I would recommend that you bring up your PowerPoint presentation, turn on the projector, and then have someone go to the back of the room and see if your slides are readable. You should also think about your audience. If your audience is older or has poor vision, a larger font may be needed.

Should you give your audience handouts of the PowerPoint presentation? I generally do not recommend that. Handouts take away the audience's attention from your speech, just as heavily worded slides do. Apart from putting small amounts of information on your slides and using a large font, another rule to follow is that you should never use all capital letters on your slides. You can capitalize the start of a sentence or for individual words that need to be capitalized, but don't put an entire sentence in capitals as it is often more difficult to read that way. Also, don't abbreviate any more than you absolutely need to, because it will only confuse Iudience more and defeat the puffect effectively delivering information.

Another good rule for PowerPoint slides is to add in pictures or videos that illustrate your experiment and bring it to life. Be sure to have a brief caption or title on the slide with any pictures or videos that you include along with a reference, if needed. It is also acceptable to make a slide with more than one picture on it; just be sure to fit them to a reasonable size on the slide. The nice thing about pictures is that they can capture and create a feeling or emotion that cannot be easily done with words. Videos are helpful too if they are short, fun to watch, and directly related to your experiment. You can show the experiment room you used or the apparatus that brought your experiment to life. On that note, be careful not to break any confidentiality laws by showing your participants' faces or names in any videos or photographs. Also, make sure to test out your sound before the presentation begins so that you know your video will play properly.

When you are ready to present the results section from your presentation, one of the most important things that you can do with slides is to put your tables and graphs on them using APA formatting. Results can be illustrated with a *t*-table, ANOVA table, or various other types of tables and/or charts. As a researcher who has watched hundreds of presentations, I find that the most important slides are the ones that show that the experiment worked. It's easy for a researcher to make claims about their research findings, but until they actually show the statistics and let the audience study them, the results won't be truly understood or accepted. Researchers need evidence that they can examine in order to be convinced of its truth; this is just the nature of a researcher's way of thinking. You will want to avoid putting raw data into your slides (or your paper), as it is not meaningful to your audience. What you want to report are your overall statistical results, which we discussed more extensively in Chapter 9.

As a final note, color is also very important in a presentation. I would advise using some color and avoid using only gray scale for your slides, as it is drab and boring. Be sure to use colors and contrasts that are easy to read, avoiding designs that are too bold or distracting. Few things are more frustrating in a presentation than staring at a slide that can't be read or understood. Simplicity is a good approach here.

Poster Presentations

There are fewer rules when it comes to creating a poster presentation, along with some particular limitations. There is less that you can do to communicate your research when you use a poster. The basic idea of a poster is that most, if not all, of your research goes onto the poster, despite its lack of size compared to a PowerPoint presentation. You might get up to one minute to talk to a very small audience that passes by your poster, but that's about it. The good news about posters is that they are a lot less stressful to present because they take less time, and you usually don't have to stand and speak in front of a large audience.

The home page of Muhlenberg College (2020) provides some good tips for creating a poster presentation. The most important tip is to be sure you have all sections of your paper, such as the abstract, introduction, methods, results, discussion, references, tables, and appendices (if relevant), on your poster. Muhlenberg also recommends that you use a large font and a nice color for your pages and/or background poster. Be sure to arrange the sections of your report from top to bottom (see the illustration in Figure 13.2), and don't put too much information on your poster.

SAMPLE IMAGE FOR A PSYCHOLOGY RESEARCH POSTER

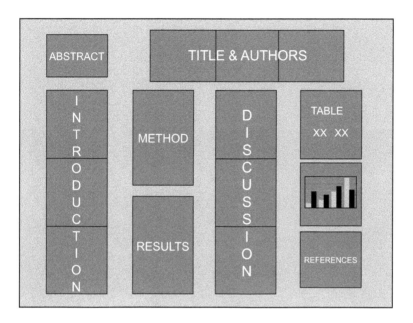

Whether you are giving a speech with a PowerPoint presentation or a poster, keep in mind that nobody knows this study like you do. You are the expert, just like a professor. Give your speech with confidence, and have fun sharing your knowledge.

References

Goodreads Inc. (2020). *Jerry Seinfeld Quotes*. www.goodreads.com/author/quotes/19838. Jerry_Seinfeld

Muhlenberg College. (2020). *Poster Presentation*. www.muhlenberg.edu/academics/psychology/posterpresentation/

14 Conclusion

What Might Be in Your Future?

Congratulations – you have now finished your senior thesis project! Now comes the question that you will be asked many times: What are you going to do next? What will you do with a bachelor's degree in psychology? This chapter explores that question and looks at several options that you have.

Because you completed a senior honors thesis, this shows that you are driven and ambitious. It is very possible that you want a traditional career in psychology, such as becoming a professor, researcher, therapist, or consultant. Let's look at these options first.

Professor. In order to become a professor of psychology, you will need a minimum of a master's degree, but a PhD is preferred. If you would like to teach at a community college, you can teach with a master's. But if you want to teach at a four-year college or a university, a doctorate is needed. You will also make

DOI: 10.4324/9781003099406-17

more money with a doctorate. Keep in mind that a doctorate is 4–5 years of very challenging work. You may often find yourself working more than 12 hours a day. It's a degree that will change you in many ways because of the discipline that is required to finish it. But this degree will put you at the top of your field. Also, there are so many different areas of psychology where you can earn a doctorate, and they will all need teachers. Be sure to check out the "divisions" page at the apa.org website to learn about all the different areas of psychology. Some of the best fields to study now are biological psychology (neuroscience) and cognitive psychology. Experience with statistics and research methods will also help you get a job in these areas.

Researcher. Many people finish their doctorate degree and get a job as a full-time researcher (nonteaching). You may work in a university or for a research institute such as a think tank, or the U.S. Government General Accounting Office. Many pure research jobs are "soft money." This means that you need to bring in your own grant money so you have a salary. That is not ideal for everyone. One of the most popular "hard money" (salaried) jobs is working as a program evaluator. Every time an agency creates a program, such as food stamps, drug reduction programs, or a new curriculum, a third-party researcher needs to be hired to see if the program works. A program evaluator usually uses their research methods and statistics skills to see how well a program is working and where it needs to be changed. They typically get paid well, too.

With the rise of social media sites that are often funded by advertising, there is a newer type of research position that is very popular and pays very well. You can work in data analytics for a research or analytics company. Social media sites often employ data analysts, or they use third-party research companies. For these jobs, you will need the statistics courses you took as part of your doctorate, and you will also need to know how to use statistical computer software.

Therapist/clinical psychologist: A lot of people who major in psychology want to go to graduate school so that they can become a therapist. There are various different types of therapists out there, and the titles and requirements vary by state and country. In the state of California, one of the most popular degrees is an MFT, a master's in marriage and family therapy. When you complete this two-year graduate degree, you then enroll in a 3,000-hour internship where you work as a supervised therapist. After you complete your internship, you take the licensing exam. When you pass the exam, you can work as a licensed therapist. A similar degree, called an MSW or a master's in social work, also requires a two-year graduate degree, internship, and licensing exam. The coursework, though, is quite different for the MSW, as are the skills learned.

Many people decide that they want to get a doctoral degree right after completing their bachelors or master's degree so that they can become a licensed clinical psychologist. This typically requires a five-year doctoral degree (usually a PhD, PsyD, and sometimes an EdD) in clinical psychology as well as an internship and licensing exam. A clinical psychologist has more training and skills than an MFT and will also earn a higher salary. The requirements for this position are much tougher than those for the MFT or LCSW.

Consultant: A consultant is a broad term for anyone who has an education and strong skills in a certain area and would like to guide others so that they can attain more success. In psychology, you often find consultants in the area of industrial and organizational psychology, and sometimes in statistics and research methods. Most consultants are "external"; they don't work for a major company but rather start their own business and market their skills to companies that need their help. Bigger companies often have "internal" consultants who are employed by the company and work only for that one company.

Working as a professor, therapist, researcher, or consultant are the most common jobs attained by people with a master's or doctoral degree in psychology. However, there are also several different options for psychology related jobs if you have just a bachelor's degree. Here are some of those options.

Research assistant
Psychiatric aide or attendant
Counseling
Correctional treatment specialist
Human resources assistant or advisor
Research analyst
Cognitive-behavioral health specialist (I/DD community)
Project evaluator
Technical writer

These are just some of the jobs you may find available to you, as there are also many other types of jobs (including those outside the realm of psychology) that you may become eligible for once you graduate with a four-year degree:

Police or parole officer
Life coach
Criminal investigator
Public relations representative
Preschool teacher
Special education teacher

My co-author Lindsay found a job she never thought she would go into after graduating with a bachelor's degree in psychology. She was all set to attend her undergraduate college for their master's program in the fall, when she was offered a job as a direct support professional for individuals with intellectual/developmental disabilities in Oregon. Although it was a difficult decision to make, she chose to relocate to Oregon to begin the new job instead of continuing straight into graduate school. She was initially placed in a group home, but when that wasn't the right fit for her, they soon found her another setting that worked better. Sometimes the job you go into right after graduating college isn't quite the one you expected. But Lindsay and I have both found that it is the unexpected happenstances that can end up being the most meaningful.

Index

Note: Page numbers in *italic* indicate a figure and page numbers in **bold** indicate a table on the corresponding page.

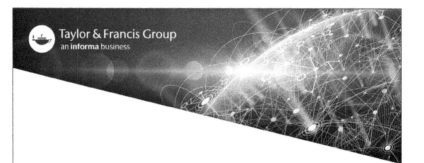